RENAISSANCE

VOLUME 8

Palestrina — Reformation

GROLIER
EDUCATIONAL

Published by Grolier Educational
Sherman Turnpike
Danbury, Connecticut 06816

© 2002 Brown Partworks Limited

Set ISBN 0-7172-5673-1
Volume 8 ISBN 0-7172-5670-7

Library of Congress Cataloging-in-Publication Data

Renaissance.
     p. cm.
Summary: Chronicles the cultural and artistic flowering
known as the Renaissance that flourished in Europe and
in other parts of the world from approximately 1375 to
1575 A.D.
Includes index.
Contents: v. 1. Africa–Bologna — v. 2. Books and libraries–
Constantinople — v. 3. Copernicus–Exploration — v. 4.
Eyck–Government — v. 5. Guilds and crafts–Landscape
painting — v. 6. Language–Merchants — v. 7. Michelangelo–
Palaces and villas — v. 8. Palestrina–Reformation — v. 9.
Religious dissent–Tapestry — v. 10. Technology–Zwingli.
  ISBN 0-7172-5673-1 (set : alk. paper)
  1. Renaissance—Juvenile literature. [1. Renaissance.]
I. Grolier Educational (Firm)
  CB361 .R367 2002
  940.2'1—dc21
                          2002002477

For information address the publisher:
Grolier Educational, Sherman Turnpike,
Danbury, Connecticut 06816

FOR BROWN PARTWORKS

Project Editor:	Shona Grimbly
Deputy Editor:	Rachel Bean
Text Editors:	Chris King
	Jane Scarsbrook
Designer:	Sarah Williams
Picture Research:	Veneta Bullen
Maps:	Colin Woodman
Design Manager:	Lynne Ross
Production:	Matt Weyland
Managing Editor:	Tim Cooke
Consultant:	Stephen A. McKnight
	University of Florida

Printed and bound in Singapore

ABOUT THIS BOOK

This is one of a set of 10 books that tells the story of the Renaissance—a time of discovery and change in the world. It was during this period—roughly from 1375 to 1575—that adventurous mariners from Europe sailed the vast oceans in tiny ships and found the Americas and new sea routes to the Spice Islands of the East. The influx of gold and silver from the New World and the increase in trade made many merchants and traders in Europe extremely rich. They spent some of their wealth on luxury goods like paintings and gold and silver items for their homes, and this created a new demand for the work of artists of all kinds. Europe experienced a cultural flowering as great artists like Leonardo da Vinci, Michelangelo, and Raphael produced masterpieces that have never been surpassed.

At the same time, scholars were rediscovering the works of the ancient Greek and Roman writers, and this led to a new way of looking at the world based on observation and the importance of the individual. This humanism, together with other new ideas, spread more rapidly than ever before thanks to the development of printing with movable type.

There was upheaval in the church too. Thinkers such as Erasmus and Luther began to question the teachings of the established church, and this eventually led to a breakaway from the Catholic church and the setting up of Protestant churches—an event called the Reformation.

The set focuses on Europe, but it also looks at how societies in other parts of the world such as Africa, China, India, and the Americas were developing, and the ways in which the Islamic and Christian worlds interacted.

The entries in this set are arranged alphabetically and are illustrated with paintings, photographs, drawings, and maps, many from the Renaissance period. Each entry ends with a list of cross-references to other entries in the set, and at the end of each book there is a timeline to help you relate events to one another in time.

There is also a useful "Further Reading" list that includes websites, a glossary of special terms, and an index covering the whole set.

Contents

VOLUME 8

Palestrina

Above: A 16th-century portrait of Palestrina by an unknown artist. Palestrina was a prolific composer of church music at a time when the church was seeking to simplify the complex music of its past.

Giovanni Pierluigi da Palestrina (about 1525–1594) was one of the greatest composers of the late 16th century. He wrote more than 100 masses, nearly 400 motets (short unaccompanied choral works), and a quantity of madrigals (part songs for several voices). He was noted for his mastery of polyphony, in which several strands of music are intertwined, and the clarity of his masses earned him the approval of the Catholic church when it was seeking to improve the quality of church music.

Palestrina was born in the cathedral town of Palestrina near Rome. While still a child, he was taken to Rome, where he studied music and sang in a church choir. He returned home in 1544 to become the cathedral organist, a post he combined with singing in the choir and teaching music. He married in 1547 and had three sons.

SUCCESS IN ROME

In 1550 the bishop of Palestrina was made Pope Julius III; and when he moved to Rome, he took his young employee with him to be director of music at the Julian Chapel of Saint Peter's Cathedral. But Julius died soon after, and the new pope, Paul IV, dismissed Palestrina. The young musician soon found another post at the church of Saint John Lateran, and there he wrote his *Improperia* ("Reproaches"), a series of chants to be sung on Good Friday. This music attracted the attention of the pope, who liked it so much that he had it performed in the Sistine Chapel—where it would be performed every Holy Week for the next 300 years.

By 1567 Palestrina was working as music director for Cardinal Ippolito d'Este, a wealthy patron of the arts. A good deal of his music had been published by this time, and he was now much in demand. In 1571 he returned to Rome, where he remained for the rest of his life.

Palestrina lived during the time of the Counter Reformation, when the Catholic church started to reject the difficult, complex music of its past. It now wanted simple, straightforward music with singable melodies and readily understandable words. Palestrina's compositional skills were such that he was able to write the kind of music the church required without any loss of beauty or artistry. His polyphonic masses were renowned for their seamlessly blended texture, in which all the separate voices were perfectly balanced. He was so highly esteemed by the church that in 1577 he was asked to edit and rewrite the church's books of plainsong along the new guidelines.

EFFORTLESS FLOW

Almost all of Palestrina's music was for the church. His music was noted for its gentle, effortless flow, rising and falling without sudden breaks or any of the dissonances (clashing notes) beloved of some of his contemporaries. He was a practical composer and was always aware of the limitations of the voices for which he was writing. Notes were never too high or too low, nor did the musical phrases require excessively long breaths. Palestrina's music served as a model for his fellow composers and for all church composers right to the present day.

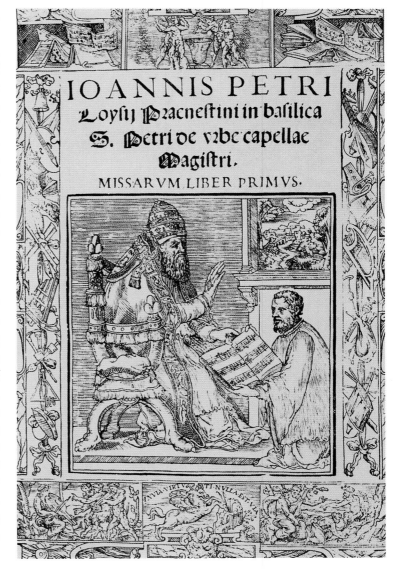

Above: The title page of Palestrina's first book of masses, showing him presenting the work to Pope Julius III.

POLYPHONY

The word "polyphony" comes from a Greek word meaning "many sounds." It describes music in which two or more melodies, or strands, are blended together. Although they are blended, all the melodies are equally important, and all are intended to be heard clearly. A special feature of polyphony is "imitation," when one voice or instrument echoes another by repeating a melody or short phrase.

Polyphony developed in the ninth century, when composers of church music—who had previously only written single-line plainsong—began to look for ways of making their music more varied. Polyphonic music was at its height in the late Renaissance period, when Palestrina was writing his greatest works. In the baroque period polyphony came to be associated with instrumental rather than vocal music and was known under a new name—counterpoint—to distinguish it from earlier polyphony.

SEE ALSO
♦ Counter Reformation
♦ Monteverdi
♦ Music
♦ Saint Peter's, Rome

Palladio

Andrea Palladio (1508–1580) was the most famous Italian architect of the second half of the 16th century and one of the most influential figures in the history of Western architecture. He is best remembered for his villas (country houses) designed in a "classical" style inspired by ancient Roman architecture and for his treatise (book) *I quattro libri dell' architettura* ("The Four Books of Architecture").

Palladio was born in Padua and carried out most of his work in the nearby city of Vicenza. He trained as a stonemason and in about 1538 began work at a villa on the outskirts of Vicenza belonging to Count Gian Giorgio Trissino, a humanist scholar, poet, and amateur architect. Trissino was impressed by Palladio and became his friend and patron. He also gave him the name "Palladio," derived from Pallas Athena, a Greek goddess and patroness of the arts (his real name was Andrea della Pietro della Gondola).

Trissino had a keen interest in the architecture of ancient Rome—he was remodeling his villa in the "classical," or ancient Roman, style—and encouraged Palladio to study the subject. Under his guidance Palladio read the influential treatise written by the Roman architect Vitruvius and studied the remains of Roman buildings. The two men went to Rome in 1541, where they examined ancient ruins and also the work of Renaissance architects like Bramante. Palladio was greatly influenced by the grandeur of both the ancient and the Renaissance architecture that he saw. He returned to the city many times.

Palladio now combined the practical skills he had learned as a mason with an understanding of the theories of classical architecture and contemporary fashions in Rome. From the late 1540s he was in constant demand as an architect. The first milestone in his career was the remodeling of the 15th-century

Below: Palladio's most famous building, the Villa Rotunda (1565–1569), which stands on a small hill outside Vicenza. It was built as a summer house for Paolo Almerico, a wealthy church official, and its classical features and harmonious design influenced generations of architects.

town hall in Vicenza, which he began in 1548. He went on to design other public buildings, several palaces, and a theater in Vicenza, and two churches in Venice: San Giorgio Maggiore (begun 1575) and Il Redentore (begun 1577). However, he is remembered above all for his villas, about 20 of which survive.

PALLADIO'S VILLAS

Villas became popular in the countryside around Venice and Vicenza in the second half of the 16th century, when wealthy city-dwellers had them built either as the centers of farms or as country retreats. Palladio's designs were influenced by traditional farm buildings in the area but most of all by what he thought ancient Roman villas looked like. He gave his villas grand porticoes (roofed entrance structures) based on ancient Roman temple fronts, which consisted of a large base on top of which columns supported a low triangular gable called a pediment. Palladio thought that ancient Roman houses as well as temples had impressive entrances like these, a belief that experts now know was mistaken.

In addition to planning villas with classical features, Palladio also designed them according to Renaissance ideas on harmony. Harmony was considered an important quality in buildings; and Palladio, like other architects, tried to attain it by using certain proportions and shapes—principally the cube and sphere—that were considered ideal or perfect. All Palladio's villas are based on the cube. His best-known building, the Villa Rotunda (begun 1565) just outside Vicenza, is a cube with a dome on top and has a magnificent portico on each side.

Palladio established a reputation for himself not only with his buildings but also through his books, and one of

them, *I quattro libri dell' architettura* (1570), ensured his lasting influence. Inspired by Vitruvius and the writings of other Renaissance architects, it laid out his ideas on classical architecture and showed how classical rules could be applied to modern requirements. It was illustrated with drawings and plans, many showing his own buildings, which other architects were able to adapt for their own purposes.

Palladio's imposing, harmonious classical style with its beautiful detailing had a lasting influence on architecture. The 17th-century architect Inigo Jones introduced the "Palladian" style to England, and in the 18th century it flourished across Europe. It also spread to America, where Thomas Jefferson modeled his house at Monticello in Virginia (begun in 1770) on the Villa Rotunda.

Above: A room in Palladio's Villa Barbaro at Maser (about 1560). The villa has one of the finest interiors of the period, with painted decorations by Paolo Veronese.

SEE ALSO

♦ Antiquities
♦ Architecture
♦ Classicism
♦ Drama and Theater
♦ Palaces and Villas
♦ Theories of Art and Architecture

Papacy

The leader of the Roman Catholic church is called the pope, from the Latin word *papa,* the title given to bishops. The papacy refers both to the office held by the pope and also to the central government of the Roman Catholic church. Today Roman Catholics consider the pope infallible (incapable of being wrong in religious matters), but in Renaissance times he was simply thought of as the head of the church. Some people even thought that church councils should be able to make decisions that could overrule the pope. Many Renaissance popes were more concerned with ruling their lands in central Italy than with the spiritual authority of the church.

By the 13th century the popes were powerful temporal (political) leaders as well as religious ones. They ruled land in central Italy known as the Papal States, covering much of the Italian provinces of Lazio, Umbria, the Marches, and Romagna, together with a small territory in southern France known as the Comtat Venaissin.

In order to run the affairs of the church and the Papal States, the medieval papacy needed a large administration. This papal government was called the curia. The most powerful members of the curia were cardinals (churchmen ranking just below the pope). The cardinals together formed a body known as the Sacred College of Cardinals. From the 12th century the College of Cardinals had the right to elect a new pope from among its own

number. Cardinals usually kept lavish palaces and large numbers of followers. For example, Cardinal Francesco Gonzaga—a member of the ruling Gonzaga family of Mantua—had a retinue of 80 members.

WEAKNESS AND CORRUPTION

The curia cost the papacy a great deal of money, and the papacy raised funds by selling indulgences (pardons for sins) and benefices (church positions). Corruption was rife, bringing the church and the papacy into disrepute. One English reformer, John Wycliffe (1330–1384), criticized the pope's luxurious lifestyle and objected to

Above: A 15th-century painting showing Pope Sixtus IV (pope 1471–1484) appointing the Vatican librarian. Sixtus encouraged learning and added a great number of books to the Vatican library. He also established the first foundling hospital and built many churches.

paying papal taxes. A Bohemian follower of Wycliffe, Jan Hus, continued the barrage of criticism and was burned for his beliefs in 1415.

Early Renaissance popes showed little interest in reform to counter these criticisms, fearing that it would weaken their power. Instead, the papacy relied on the rigorous trial and punishment of critics and troublemakers. Over the centuries the papacy had developed its own body of laws (known as canon law), and there was a busy papal law court. Another court, called the Inquisition, was founded in 1231 and was used to search out and to try heretics—people whom the church accused of going against church dogma, that is, its established beliefs.

FROM ROME TO AVIGNON

In 1309 the papacy fell under the control of the French king Philip IV, who forced the pope to move from Rome to Avignon, a city in the Comtat Venaissin. This move was opposed by the Italians, and it antagonized Eng-land and Germany, which were fearful of France's influence on the papacy. It was almost 70 years before the papacy returned to Rome in 1378, and even then serious conflict arose.

THE GREAT SCHISM

The newly elected pope, Urban VI (pope 1378–1389), made enemies of the College of Cardinals through his efforts to reform abuses in the church. The cardinals declared his appointment invalid and elected another pope, Clement VII (pope 1378–1394). Urban refused to yield the papacy and remained in Rome, while the rival pope moved to Avignon—his enemies called him the antipope. For 39 years there were two popes, each claiming to be the rightful head of the church. This long dispute, which seriously undermined the authority of the pope and the church, was known as the Great Schism. It was not until 1417, when the Council of Constance elected a new pope, Martin V (pope 1417–1431), that the schism finally came to an end.

Left: A detail from a 15th-century painting showing Pope Martin V in procession through the streets of Siena. Martin V was elected by the Council of Constance in 1417 to put an end to the Great Schism.

In the second half of the 15th century and the early 16th century a series of ambitious popes began to rebuild the papacy's power. They worked hard to return the city of Rome to its former grandeur and make it an impressive center of the Roman Catholic church. They also wooed the ruling families of Europe. Every year, for example, the pope sent a golden sword and rose to the prince or city that had done the most for the church.

CENTER OF DIPLOMACY

Rome also became Europe's most important center for diplomacy, and the curia was often thronged with ambassadors. The popes of the early 16th century also involved themselves in forging political alliances and waging war to maintain and expand their territorial power.

The popes' determination to hold onto their lands in Italy involved them in war with France, Spain, and the Holy Roman Empire, as well as neighboring independent city-states. Pope Julius II (pope 1503–1513) was an enthusiastic soldier. In 1506 he attacked the cities of Bologna and Perugia, which had declared themselves independent. The spectacle of the pope at war with Catholic subjects showed the whole of Europe that the papacy took its political position more seriously than its spiritual role.

The papacy had no standing army and so depended on mercenaries (hired soldiers). Often popes would make alliances to achieve their goals rather

POPES AS PATRONS

The popes were important supporters and patrons of Renaissance art and culture. They were often inspired by a mixture of religious and political motives. In the early 1430s, for example, Pope Eugenius IV (pope 1431–1447) asked the Florentine sculptor Filarete (1400–1469) to make a pair of bronze doors for the basilica (church) of Saint Peter's in Rome. The doors depicted scenes from the life of Saint Peter, but Filarete also included in the design the arms of Eugenius's family, the Condulmer.

In the early 16th century Rome and the papal court became the new center of Italian Renaissance art and architecture. Julius II (pope 1503–1513) employed the architect Bramante to lay out a new plan for the city, including the Via Giulia—the first great street built since ancient Roman times—as well as a new Saint Peter's. Julius also summoned numerous artists to the city, including Raphael and Michelangelo, to decorate the papal palaces.

Right: The west door of Saint Peter's, designed by Filarete for Pope Eugenius IV. The door shows Saint Peter giving the keys of the city to the pope.

Left: A mid 16th-century painting of the Venetian school showing a session of the Council of Trent (1545–1563) held in the cathedral of San Vigilio. The Council of Trent launched the Counter Reformation in an attempt to combat Protestantism and stamp out abuses in the church.

than go to war. For example, Leo X (pope 1513–1521) signed a concordat (treaty) in 1516 with the French king Francis I giving Francis a say in the choice of bishops in return for keeping French troops out of papal lands.

SACK OF ROME

In 1527 the papacy was humiliated when the troops of the Holy Roman emperor Charles V sacked (captured and plundered) Rome. Many of the emperor's soldiers were Protestant mercenaries who had not been paid, and in anger they looted, murdered, and dragged elderly cardinals through the streets. When the pope called for Romans to defend their city, only a few hundred responded. The event stunned Europe, but many people thought it was God's way of punishing the worldly papacy. The sack of Rome, combined with the threat of Prot-estantism, finally convinced the papacy that it was time to reform.

The rise of Protestantism in the early 16th century led to the Reformation. Reformers such as Martin Luther in Germany and Huldrych Zwingli in Switzerland challenged not only the religious leadership of the papacy but also its political authority. Early critics of the papacy, such as William of Ockham, had argued that the pope and the church should have no role at all in political affairs. Some Protestants now took up these arguments and criticized what they saw as the corruption of the Roman church.

The papacy responded by launching the Counter Reformation to reform the Roman Catholic church and attack the new Protestantism. A council of church leaders held at the northern Italian city of Trent from 1545 to 1563 reasserted traditional Catholic dogma and took measures to stamp out corruption and abuse. The Council of Trent launched a new, strengthened papacy that was ready to meet the challenges of both Protestantism and the expansion of Christianity into the newly discovered lands of the Americas.

Papal States

During the Renaissance the pope was not only the spiritual leader of the Catholic church but also a political leader and great landowner who ruled over large territories in central Italy. These possessions were known as the Papal States, and the popes governed them for more than 1,000 years, from 754 to 1870.

The exact area ruled by the pope changed continually over the centuries, as did the amount of power that he realistically held over his lands. Broadly speaking, however, the states formed a diagonal belt that stretched across the Italian peninsula, approximately from Rome in the south to Ravenna in the north. At various times this area included the cities of Urbino, Ancona, Parma, Piacenza, Spoleto, and Perugia.

The Papal States were based on lands given to Pope Stephen II (died 757) by the powerful Frankish king Pepin III in 754. The popes of the Middle Ages spent a lot of their time organizing armies, raising money, and seeking allies to help them protect these lands from their enemies—especially the Holy Roman emperors in Germany. The popes also had to contend with the rise of strong communal governments and powerful local families. When the center of papal

Below: Morning parade of the Swiss Guard at the Vatican Palace. The Swiss Guard is a corps of bodyguards that was set up to protect the pope—membership is limited to natives of Switzerland. Vatican City is all that remains today of the pope's possessions in Italy—the former Papal States.

power moved to the French city of Avignon in 1309, the popes lost control of many of their lands in Italy.

PROBLEMS AT HOME

It was not until the early 15th century that popes were able to turn their attention to the problems of controlling their lands at home. By this time the political situation in the Papal States was extremely complicated. Often nobles ruled cities as vicars in the pope's name, but acted as if they were independent from Rome. There were great rivalries between different families, factions, and cities, and popes had to exploit these conflicts to bring rebellious rulers back under their control. Popes therefore had to be highly skilled politicians as well as spiritual leaders.

One such pope was Martin V (pope 1417–1431). Before Martin's reign there had been a split in the church known as the Great Schism, in which there were two popes. Under Martin the papacy was unified again, which allowed the pope to concentrate on political matters. The new pope slowly began to bring order to the Papal States, making shrewd diplomatic alliances and placing family members in important positions.

MILITARY POPES

Later popes used military force to expand the territory under their command. Among the most famous were Alexander VI (pope 1492–1503) and Julius II (pope 1503–1513). Alexander's armies were led by his illegitimate son Cesare Borgia, who in a series of military campaigns brought cities such as Rimini and Urbino under papal control. Alexander was succeeded by Julius II, who often personally led his armies. He managed to take

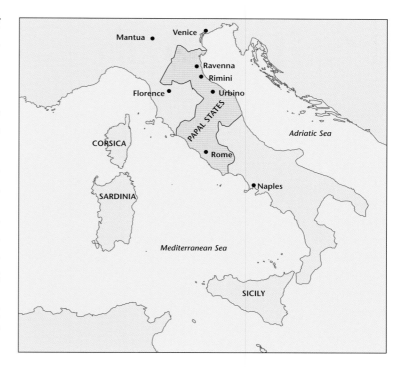

Ravenna and other city-states from Venice and later also claimed the cities of Parma and Piacenza.

It was during Julius's reign that the Papal States reached their greatest geographical size. Along with Milan, Florence, Naples, and Venice the Papal States were one of the five major powers in Italy. However, Alexander's and Julius's preoccupation with political matters had serious consequences for the Catholic church. Their worldliness and neglect of religious issues led to much resentment. This resentment was a major factor behind the Protestant Reformation.

The importance of the Papal States as an independent region declined in the 16th century, and by the end of the century the papal territory was just one of the many minor Italian states. The Papal States continued to exist until the creation of modern Italy in 1870. Yet even then the popes were allowed to continue to govern Vatican City in central Rome, which is still technically an independent state today.

Above: A map showing the extent of the Papal States in the early 16th century. Controlling the Papal States took up much time and energy, diverting the attention of the popes from spiritual matters.

SEE ALSO

♦ Alexander VI
♦ Borgia Family
♦ Catholic Church
♦ Julius II
♦ Martin V
♦ Papacy
♦ Rome
♦ Urbino
♦ Venice

Paris

In the 13th century Paris was France's flourishing capital, but over the next 400 years it was to suffer many hardships. In the 14th century it was struck by the Black Death (the plague), and in the 15th century it was occupied by the English. The late 15th and early 16th centuries saw a period of prosperity, as the French kings made Paris a great Renaissance city, but in the late 16th century the Wars of Religion brought more bloodshed and unrest.

The Black Death swept through Paris in 1348–1349, killing many of its citizens, and the outbreak of the Hundred Years' War (1340–1453) between France and England brought more suffering. Parisians bore the brunt of the war costs, and in 1382 they rebelled against tax increases. Their revolt was brutally put down. French fortunes in the war took a downturn, and from 1420 to 1436 Paris came under English rule—the duke of Bedford governed the city on behalf of the English king Henry VI. Many attempts were made to drive the English out, including one led by the French heroine Joan of Arc in 1429.

However, the French and English signed a truce in 1444, which resulted in a period of peace and prosperity for Paris under the French king Charles VII. Many new mansions were built by wealthy nobles on the right (north) bank of the Seine River. The left bank was home to the university, which had grown up in the 12th century. In 1469 the first French printing press was installed at the university, and many Italian poets and thinkers made their way to the city.

AN ELEGANT CITY

By the mid-16th century Paris had become an elegant city, growing in size and influence. King Francis I, a great patron of French and Italian artists, brought Renaissance architecture to the city. He had a new Hôtel de Ville (townhall) built and in 1546 had the old fortress of the Louvre replaced with a brand-new palace, which became the royal residence.

This period of prosperity was halted by religious wars between Catholics and Huguenots (French Protestants). In 1572 about 3,000 Huguenots attending the wedding of Henry of Navarre were killed in the Saint Bartholomew's Day Massacre. The massacre sparked unrest all over France.

Above: The Louvre in Paris, which was begun in 1546 and completed in the mid-19th century. It was built for King Francis I and remained the royal residence until 1682.

SEE ALSO

♦ Architecture
♦ France
♦ Francis I
♦ French Art
♦ Joan of Arc
♦ Marguerite of Navarre
♦ Raphael
♦ Wars of Religion

Patronage

The artists and sculptors of today usually decide for themselves what they are going to paint or sculpt and produce the work in their own studio. They then try to find a buyer, either by holding a public exhibition of their works or by finding a dealer who will try to make a sale. In the Renaissance the relationship between artist and buyer was completely different. Wealthy people or organizations wanting a painting or sculpture would ask an artist to make the piece in return for a prearranged fee. This kind of buyer is known as a patron, and the system of ordering (or commissioning) art in this way is called patronage.

The patron usually laid down clear guidelines as to what sort of work he or she wanted, so that to some extent the great works of Renaissance art were the result of a partnership between the patron and artist. Wealthy patrons commissioned not only painters and sculptors but also woodworkers, goldsmiths, silversmiths, embroiderers, tapestry makers, and many other kinds of craftspeople.

TWO KINDS OF PATRON

There were two main kinds of patron: individuals and organizations. An individual patron might be a prince or duke, a powerful statesman, a rich merchant, or just a wealthy citizen. Patrons were usually men, but some of them were women. One of the greatest patrons of the Renaissance was Isabella d'Este, duchess of Mantua (1474–

1539), who commissioned paintings from the finest artists of the age, including Andrea Mantegna. Some ruling families—such as the Medici of Florence, the Gonzaga of Mantua, and

Below: The artist Michelangelo presenting a model of a palace to his patron, the pope.

the Montefeltro of Urbino—became outstanding patrons of the arts.

A princely ruler might keep a court artist, who in return for an annual salary or a series of one-time payments would carry out all kinds of commissions for his patron. His work might range from painting frescoes (wall paintings) and portraits to designing textiles for clothes or banners for festivals. As court artist to the French governor of Milan, for example, Leonardo da Vinci was expected not only to produce portraits and Madonnas (portraits or sculptures of the Virgin Mary) but also to design toys such as the mechanical lion that he made on the occasion of a visit by the French king.

Large organizations, such as the church, city governments, guilds, and hospitals, were also important patrons. In Italy many of these institutions appointed a committee called an *opera* to oversee the commissioning of buildings and artworks. Some of these *opere* became very powerful. In Florence, for example, the *opera* of the wool merchants' guild financed and oversaw the decorations for the city's cathedral. In Venice the religious brotherhoods of citizens known as the *scuole* ("schools") were by far the most important patrons in the city.

PIETY AND PROPAGANDA

Patrons commissioned artworks for many reasons. The Florentine merchant Giovanni Rucellai was one of the most lavish individual patrons of the 15th century. He ordered a chapel to be built for his local church and paid for a new façade (begun in 1458) designed by Alberti for one of Florence's main churches, Santa Maria Novella. He also filled his house with paintings and sculptures by some of the leading

artists of his age, including Paolo Uccello, Filippo Lippi, and Verrocchio. In one of his notebooks he explained why he was such a enthusiastic patron of the arts. One of his motives, he

---

The merchant Giovanni Rucellai filled his house with paintings and sculptures

---

wrote, was his pride and pleasure in spending his money so well. However, he also claimed he "wanted to serve the glory of God, the honor of the city, and the commemoration of myself."

For powerful rulers, such as the Medici, lavish expenditure on art was one way of making their subjects or fellow citizens aware of their political power. Often a complex mixture of

Below: **The Madonna of Chancellor Rolin,** *painted by Jan van Eyck (1385–1441). A donor portrait of the chancellor, left, shows him kneeling before the Virgin.*

motives—both worldly and spiritual—lay behind patronage. When Chancellor Rolin commissioned Jan van Eyck to paint *The Madonna of Chancellor Rolin*, he stipulated that he would be shown kneeling before the Virgin. Clearly, Rolin—who was a proud and ambitious statesman—wanted to show his piety in this painting, but he also wanted to show

Above: **The Procession in the Piazza San Marco,** *by Gentile Bellini (1429–1507), which was intended to show the piety and power of the* **scuola** *in Venice that commissioned it.*

what an important man he was and to make sure that future generations remembered him. A portrait of a patron included as part of a religious painting is known as a donor portrait and is a common feature of Renaissance altarpieces.

For the great organizations that commissioned artworks, piety, civic pride, and propaganda were all

 ## CONTRACTS

The contract between patron and artist was often very detailed and laid down much more than the subject, price, and completion date of the artwork. The patron often used the contract to stipulate the kind and quality of materials the artist was to use. For example, patrons often wanted painters to use precious pigments, such as powdered gold or ultramarine (a rich violet-blue made by grinding the semiprecious stone lapis lazuli), in order to demonstrate their wealth to the world. One contract made between a patron and the Florentine painter Domenico Ghirlandaio (1449–1494) stated that "the blue must be ultramarine of the value of about four florins the ounce."

By the late 15th century, however, patrons had become less interested in the materials and more in the skill of the painter. The contract for a Virgin and Child by another Florentine artist, Sandro Botticelli, stated that the artist was to be paid two florins for the ultramarine used in the painting, 38 florins for the gold, and 35 "for his brush"—that is, his skill.

Patrons often also took care to stipulate that the artist should work on the painting or sculpture personally rather than leaving the commission to his assistants. The contract for Piero della Francesca's *Madonna della Misericordia*, for example, states specifically that "no painter may put his hand to the altar other than Piero himself."

important motives. Toward the end of the 15th century the *scuola* of Saint John the Evangelist in Venice commissioned Gentile Bellini to paint *The Procession in the Piazza San Marco*. The painting shows the *scuola*'s annual procession through Venice's main square on the feast day of Saint Mark and reflects not only the religious piety of the *scuola*'s members but also their pride and power.

Sometimes patrons used art to convey more specific messages. In 1468 the leaders of the Flemish city of Louvain commissioned Dirc Bouts (about 1415–1475) to produce a series of paintings for the city hall's courtroom. The paintings illustrated stories about the medieval German emperor Otto III, who was famed for the fairness and rigor of his justice, and they were intended to impress on all the people who entered the courtroom a proper sense of awe and respect.

PATRONS AND ARTISTS

Once a patron had chosen an artist to carry out a commission, he usually gave him a description of what he expected. The patron might, for example, want an altarpiece depicting the Virgin and Child together with the patron's favorite saints. The artist then did a sketch or sometimes a model of his ideas, and the patron would approve it or ask for changes to be made. The artist and patron then signed a contract, which was a legal document setting out such things as the materials to be used, the artist's fee, and the date by which the artwork was to be finished (see box on page 17).

The artist and patron were generally on good terms, and the patron would usually leave the artist to get on with the job without interference. However, in the case of large-scale commis-

Left: **The Judgment of Otto: Ordeal by Fire**, *one of a series of 15th-century paintings by Dirc Bouts on the walls of the courtroom in the Flemish city of Louvain. By reminding people of the rigor of the German emperor Otto's justice, the paintings were intended to create an atmosphere of dignity and awe in the courtroom.*

sions—such as a series of frescoes or a large altarpiece for a church—the patron might have an ongoing influence on the work in progress. In the 1430s, for example, the *opera* of a church in the town of Borgo San Sepolcro commissioned the Sienese artist Sassetta (died about 1450) to paint an altarpiece depicting the life of Saint Francis. The altarpiece consisted of 116 different scenes, and Sassetta and the *opera* worked very closely together over a period of time to get things right.

Sometimes patrons and artists quarreled. The patron might complain that the artist was late in finishing the work or using poor-quality materials, and the artist might write to the patron asking for more money or more time. Sometimes an artist abandoned a work halfway through, and the patron had to give the work to another artist to finish.

SEE ALSO

♦ Alberti
♦ Artists'
   Workshops
♦ Bellini,
   Giovanni
♦ Eyck, Jan van
♦ Gonzaga
   Family
♦ Government,
   Systems of
♦ Guilds and
   Crafts
♦ Leonardo da
   Vinci
♦ Medici Family
♦ Painters'
   Techniques
   and Materials
♦ Portraiture
♦ Religious
   Themes in Art
♦ Tapestry
♦ Venice
♦ Wealth

Perspective

When we look at the world around us, objects appear to become smaller the farther away they are, and parallel lines—like the sidewalks of a street—appear to converge, or get closer together, as they stretch into the distance. These optical effects can be reproduced in pictures to create a lifelike sense of space using a mathematical system called linear perspective. In the 15th century Italian artists began to explore the rules of linear perspective.

Linear perspective is not the only way of suggesting depth and space in a picture. The ancient Romans, for example, used axial perspective. In this system the sides of a building are opened up rather like a stage. Other peoples did not attempt to show distance or space at all. In ancient Egyptian art artists used differently sized human figures to show their relative importance rather than the distance between them. A pharaoh or god, for example, was shown much larger than a slave.

In medieval Europe the depiction of people, objects, and space in a lifelike way was not a priority. Most paintings showed religious subjects like Christ, Mary, and the saints, and they were considered as otherworldly figures, removed from everyday life. As a result, medieval artists used rather haphazard methods of suggesting space, including axial perspective. In their paintings it often looks as if many holy figures are crammed together in a very shallow space. Although the Italian painter Giotto (1266–1337) began to modify this medieval style, linear perspective did not develop until the 15th century.

NEW ATTITUDES

Inspired by their studies of ancient Greek and Roman culture, scholars and artists began to reassess their approach to art. An important result of this reappraisal was that "naturalism," or the lifelike depiction of subjects, became desirable. This approach involved re-creating the appearance of space and distance that exists in the real world on the flat surface of a picture.

Above: Paolo Uccello's painting The Flood (about 1450) in the church of Santa Maria Novella in Florence. Uccello used perspective to add drama to this scene showing the deluge described in the story of Noah in the Old Testament.

AERIAL PERSPECTIVE

In northern Europe artists did not adopt linear perspective until the 16th century. Although artists such as Jan van Eyck (about 1385–1441) and Rogier van der Weyden (1399–1464) created paintings every bit as naturalistic as their Italian contemporaries, they used different methods to create a sense of space and distance in their work. They based their pictures on minute observation of the world, rather than the application of mathematical theories on perspective and proportion. One important technique they developed was aerial perspective. Flemish artists noted how colors farther away look paler and bluer than those close by, and imitated this subtle atmospheric effect in their work.

Above: **The Rest on the Flight into Egypt** *by an unknown Flemish painter. Aerial perspective is used to create the effect of the landscape melting into the distance.*

The Florentine architect Filippo Brunelleschi (1377–1446) was the first Renaissance artist to apply the laws of geometry to the visual world. He produced drawings in which he demonstrated that imaginary parallel lines running away from the viewer appear to converge at a single vanishing point at the viewer's eye level. Although Brunelleschi's drawings have been lost, his friend Leon Battista Alberti (about 1404–1472) set down his ideas in an influential book entitled *Della pittura* ("On painting"), published in 1435. Brunelleschi's and Alberti's early form of linear perspective is often known as *costruzione legittima* (legitimate construction) in order to distinguish it from later, more refined versions.

The first artist to put *costruzione legittima* into practice was the painter Masaccio (1401–1428). His fresco (wall painting) *The Holy Trinity* (1425) shows a group of figures in a deep and spacious chapel. The figures and the building are shown "to scale." For example, the donors (the people who paid for the painting) kneeling on a step outside the chapel are slightly larger than the holy figures inside the chapel. In a medieval painting the donors would have been shown smaller regardless of their spatial position, because they were less important.

DISPLAYS OF SKILL

Italian artists took up linear perspective with enthusiasm, and it became a key ingredient of the Renaissance style. In the eyes of many people the addition of respected subjects such as geometry to the craft of painting gave artists a new dignity. Artists competed to display the most elaborate effects of perspective.

The Florentine painter Paolo Uccello (1396/7–1475) was so obsessed by linear perspective that he stayed up late into the night making drawings of complex objects from different angles. Patrons—the people who ordered and paid for pictures—often required a painting to show a mastery of perspective as a sign of the artist's skill.

One especially prized skill was foreshortening, or the application of perspective to a single object. Sometimes artists showed off by including an arm or a leg almost at right angles to the picture plane so that it appeared strangely distorted. Uccello and the north Italian artist Andrea Mantegna were both well known for their mastery of this technique.

HARMONY AND ORDER

However, artists quickly realized that when perspective was applied as an end in itself, it did not create naturalistic pictures at all. Uccello's paintings, for

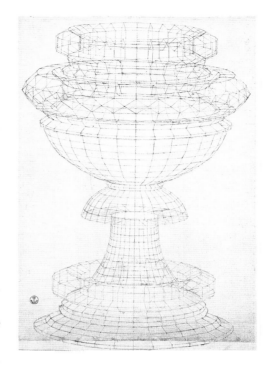

Left: A perspective drawing of a chalice by Paolo Uccello (about 1430). Uccello was fascinated by perspective, and he made many mathematical studies of objects such as this one.

example, have a fantastic quality which in part results from his rigorous use of perspective. Instead, artists saw that perspective should be used in a more understated way to impart beauty, harmony, and order to pictures. Over the years they improved and refined *costruzione legittima*.

The painter and mathematician Piero della Francesca (about 1415–1492), for example, wrote a book on perspective in which he noted that artists should avoid using the technique where it created anything that was confusing or unrecognizable. He argued that they should use perspective wisely to create a vision of clarity and grandeur.

Piero's ideas influenced generations of artists, including Leonardo da Vinci and Albrecht Dürer, both of whom wrote about perspective. Piero's ideas were perhaps most perfectly realized in Raphael's painting *The School of Athens* (see page 60), in which ancient thinkers are shown gathered in a magnificent architectural setting.

SEE ALSO

♦ Alberti
♦ Flemish Painting
♦ Landscape Painting
♦ Mantegna
♦ Masaccio
♦ Naturalism
♦ Painting
♦ Patronage
♦ Piero della Francesca
♦ Theories of Art and Architecture
♦ Uccello

Petrarch

Francesco Petrarch (1304–1374) was an Italian poet and scholar whose work had an immense influence on thought and literature during the Renaissance. He wrote poetry in both Latin and Italian, and so inspired other European writers such as the English poet Geoffrey Chaucer to write in their native, everyday language. His study of the writings and culture of ancient Greece and Rome and his search for classical manuscripts hidden away in libraries sparked enthusiasm in other scholars for their ancient heritage and founded the movement known as humanism.

Petrarch was born in Arezzo in Tuscany. When he was eight, his family moved to Avignon in the south of France, where the papal court was located after it moved there from Rome. At his father's prompting Petrarch studied law, first at Montpellier in France then at the

---

Laura inspired Petrarch to write some of the world's greatest love poetry

---

University of Bologna in Italy. However, his heart was not in his law studies. When his father died in 1326, he returned to Avignon—a move that resulted in perhaps the most important meeting of his life. On Good Friday in 1327 he saw in church a Frenchwoman named Laura, who was to inspire him to write some of the world's greatest love poetry. Although Petrarch scarcely knew her, Laura has become famous for her goodness and beauty through his poems.

STUDYING THE CLASSICS

During the 1330s Petrarch spent most of his time traveling around Europe, especially in France, Flanders, and Germany. That gave him the opportunity not only to read and write but also to track down classical manuscripts in the libraries of monasteries

Below: A 16th-century portrait of Petrarch, showing him wearing the laurel crown with which he was crowned poet laureate in a grand ceremony in Rome in 1341.

and cathedrals. Among those he found were important letters written by the ancient Roman writer and politician Cicero (106–43 B.C.). Petrarch became famous for his scholarship and verse, and in 1341 he accepted the honor of becoming the official poet, or poet laureate, of Rome. For the next few years Petrarch made his home in different Italian cities, continuing his studies and writings. He managed to escape the great plague known as the Black Death, which struck Europe in 1348 and killed his beloved Laura.

In 1350 Petrarch was in Florence, where he met his fellow poet Giovanni Boccaccio. The two men became friends, sharing an interest in the revival of classical learning. Their study of classical texts led them to reject medieval scholasticism, which they regarded as narrow and impractical. It was about this time that Petrarch campaigned for the return of the papacy from Avignon to its spiritual home—Rome.

In his later years Petrarch divided his time between Venice and Padua, where he had a house in nearby Arqua. There he died in 1374. According to one story, he passed away in his study with his head on one of his precious manuscripts: the writings of the Roman poet Virgil.

PETRARCH'S POETRY

In addition to his poems Petrarch wrote essays, dialogues, and letters, which included his thoughts on philosophy, morality, and history. Although he is best remembered for his poems in Italian, which include his poems for Laura and *Trionfi* ("The Triumphs," 1351–1374), he himself preferred the works he wrote in Latin, a language in which he expressed himself with great style and fluency. He

thought his greatest work was a long poem called *Africa*, which tells the story of the second great war fought in ancient times between the Romans and the Carthaginians, a people who lived in northern Africa.

Petrarch's most famous work is his *Rime* ("Poems"), also known as *Canzoniere* ("Song book"). It consists of 366 poems in praise of Laura and expressing the poet's love for her. They portray her as a real, living person rather than the kind of symbolic figure that earlier medieval poets tended to create when depicting women. Petrarch wrote many of the poems in a 14-line sonnet form that is named after him. This Petrarchian sonnet was to be adapted by the English poet and playwright William Shakespeare, who developed his own distinctive form of the sonnet in the late 16th century.

Above: A late 14th-century illustration for Petrarch's poem **Trionfi,** *which relates the progress of a human soul from earthly love to love of God.*

Philip II

Above: Charles V commissioned Titian to paint this portrait of his son Philip, aged 23. Philip was destined to be one of the most powerful monarchs of the Renaissance era.

Philip II of Spain (ruled 1556–1598) presided over a Spanish empire that was larger and more powerful than ever before or since. He had 16 million subjects in Europe, as well as those in Spain's overseas possessions in the Americas and the Philippines. As a devout Catholic Philip's main aim in ruling his vast empire was to keep his subjects true to the Catholic faith and fight off the threat of Protestantism that was sweeping through northern Europe. This made him a champion of the church's Counter Reformation.

Philip was born in 1527 in Valladolid, Spain, the only son of the Holy Roman emperor Charles V and Isabella of Portugal. When Charles decided to abdicate in 1555, he divided his lands between his brother Ferdinand and his son. Philip had already received the duchy of Milan and the kingdoms of Naples and Sicily, and now his father gave him the Netherlands and, in 1556, Spain and its empire. Before he died in 1558, Charles gave Philip the Franche-Comté (in the east of present-day France). In 1580 Philip claimed title to the Portuguese throne through his mother and took it by force.

A CATHOLIC KING

Philip had his first taste of power at 16, when Charles appointed him regent (caretaker ruler) of Spain in his absence. The instructions that Charles left for his son made a lasting impression. First and most important, Charles urged Philip to uphold the Roman Catholic religion and "never to let heretics into his kingdoms." To achieve this end, Philip could be a ruthless and tyrannical ruler.

In his campaign to uphold the Catholic faith Philip strengthened the Spanish Inquisition, using it to search out and burn heretics both in Spain and abroad. In 1559 the first auto da fé (public sentencing) of Protestants was held in Valladolid with Philip himself attending. Of the 25 Protestants on trial, 12 were sentenced to death. In the

THE REVOLT OF THE NETHERLANDS

When Calvinism spread to the Netherlands, Philip tried to stamp it out by using the Spanish Inquisition to interrogate, convict, and burn suspected heretics. This outraged Dutch Protestants and Catholics alike, who saw Philip's methods as an intrusion on their liberties by a foreign ruler. There were riots throughout the country, and Catholic churches were attacked. Philip sent an army of 10,000 Spanish troops under the command of the duke of Alba to suppress the uprisings, but the result was a full-scale rebellion led by Prince William of Orange, who was a stadholder, or provincial governor.

A group of Calvinist pirates called the Sea Beggars captured the northern town of Brille in Holland in 1572. They were joined by William of Orange, and the rebels soon gained control of the northern provinces of the Netherlands. In 1579 the northern provinces signed the Union of Utrecht and declared themselves an independent nation—at war with Spain. The war was still unresolved at Philip's death. Eventually, in 1648 the Netherlands were split, with Calvinism becoming the religion of the northern provinces (present-day Holland) and Catholicism that of the south (present-day Belgium).

Netherlands Philip used the Spanish Inquisition to try to stamp out Calvinism (a form of Protestantism founded by John Calvin), provoking a revolt against Spanish rule. The Inquisition was also used to punish the Moriscos (Muslims who had converted to Christianity) in southern Spain after their rebellion in 1568.

In 1554 Philip married the Catholic queen of England, Mary I, and became joint sovereign of England; but the marriage was unpopular with most of the English people. When Mary died in 1558, Philip attempted to marry her sister and successor, the Protestant Elizabeth I, but she refused him. Philip was by this time king of Spain, and from 1559 he never set foot outside the Iberian Peninsula (the region of Spain and Portugal) again.

FOREIGN POLICY
Philip had inherited a war with France from his father. He made peace in 1559 with the treaty of Cateau-Cambrésis, marrying the French princess Elizabeth of Valois to confirm the deal. Philip worked to maintain peaceful relations with his European neighbors for the

first half of his reign. This was partly because his own experience of war at the battle of Saint Quentin against the French in 1557 had given him a horror of warfare. Other reasons were that he was short of money and that he was engaged in a series of wars with the Ottoman Turks—he finally defeated them at the battle of Lepanto in 1571.

From the 1570s, however, Spanish policy began to change. The revolt of the Netherlands, which began in 1566, and the spread of Protestantism in

Below: This 16th-century picture painted on a wall plaque shows Philip making peace with Henry II of France. The two monarchs signed the treaty of Cateau-Cambrésis in 1559, ending 60 years of conflict.

Left: A painting by an unknown artist of Philip II's Escorial palace near Madrid. The building served as Philip's residence and administrative headquarters as well as being a monastery and a burial chamber for Philip's father, Charles V. When Philip died, he too was buried there.

northern Europe pushed Philip into a crusading frame of mind. When the English gave their support to the Dutch rebels, Philip made an attempt to invade Protestant England by sending his great Armada in 1588. This supposedly invincible Spanish fleet was defeated and driven back to Spain by the English. French Protestants had also supported the Dutch rebels, again provoking Philip's displeasure. Philip intervened in the French Wars of Religion and put pressure on the Protestant Henry of Navarre to become Catholic before he became king of France in 1598.

RULING FROM MADRID

When Philip settled permanently in Spain in 1559, he chose Madrid as his capital because the climate was said to be good for gout (an illness that affects the joints), from which he suffered. He decided to build a great monastery at a village called El Escorial, about 26 miles (42km) from Madrid. It was intended to be a burial place for Charles V and all succeeding Spanish monarchs. It was also to be a palace for Philip and the center of his government.

Work on this austere building began in 1563 and was completed in 1584. Philip commissioned teams of painters and sculptors, many of them Italians, to decorate the interior of the palace. It was from the Escorial that Philip ran his vast empire.

In his offices at the Escorial Philip read and made notes on nearly every document his government generated. He was painfully slow at making decisions. Philip's official court historian Cabrera de Córdoba wrote that the emperor would hold onto important papers "until they wilted."

COLD AND CRUEL?

After his death in 1598 Philip was remembered as a Catholic monster in Protestant countries. It was said that he was cold and cruel, and there were rumors that he had murdered political rivals. However, Philip was dearly loved in his native Castile, and his letters to the two daughters he had with his third wife, Elizabeth of Valois, reveal a doting father. With his fourth wife, Anne of Austria (whom he married in 1570, after Elizabeth's death), he had one son, who became Philip III of Spain.

SEE ALSO

♦ Americas
♦ Calvin
♦ Charles V
♦ Counter Reformation
♦ Elizabeth I
♦ France
♦ Hapsburg Family
♦ Inquisition
♦ Netherlands
♦ Ottoman Empire
♦ Portugal
♦ Protestantism
♦ Spain

Piero della Francesca

Piero della Francesca (about 1415–1492) was an Italian painter whose work illustrates the new developments that were taking place in art during the early Renaissance (a period spanning about 1420 to 1500). He painted in a clear, serene style and explored the newly discovered technique of perspective, a mathematical system that helps artists depict space.

Not a great deal is known about Piero's life, and only a fairly small number of paintings by him survive. Although he was highly regarded in the 15th and 16th centuries, he was largely forgotten by later generations of artists, a neglect made worse by the fact that many of his paintings were in out-of-the-way places. However, scholars studying Renaissance art in the 19th century "rediscovered" his paintings, and since that time Piero has been regarded as a key figure in the early Renaissance.

EARLY LIFE
Piero was born in Sansepolcro, a town about 95 miles (150km) from Florence. His father was a tanner and a shoemaker, and appears to have been wealthy enough to provide Piero with a good education. Nothing is known of Piero's artistic training, although by 1439 he was working with the painter Domenico Veneziano on some frescoes (wall paintings) in Florence.

At that time Florence was the center of new developments taking place in art, as painters and sculptors began to produce more naturalistic (lifelike)

works of art inspired by classical (ancient Greek and Roman) examples. Piero would have seen the sculptures of Donatello and the paintings of Masaccio and Fra Angelico, and he would have encountered the theories of the scholar and architect Leon Battista Alberti, who wrote about new ideas on art in his book *Della Pittura* ("On Painting") published in 1436.

Above: Piero della Francesca's **The Baptism of Christ** *(1450s). Piero set the scene in hilly countryside—he was one of the first Italian artists to paint realistic landscapes.*

From the 1440s Piero worked in a number of towns and cities, but he always returned to Sansepolcro, where he played a key role in civic affairs—he was elected a town councillor in 1442 and 1467. When not in Sansepolcro, Piero worked in Rome and smaller cities, including Rimini, Ferrara, and Urbino, which were thriving centers of art and culture. His largest surviving series of frescoes is in Arezzo, a town near Sansepolcro. It illustrates the legend of the True Cross, a collection of stories about the history of the cross on which Christ was crucified.

Piero painted some of his best-known pictures in Urbino, where he worked for Duke Federico da Montefeltro, a powerful condottiere (mercenary soldier) who transformed

---

Clear outlines, bright lighting, pure colors, and a sense of stillness characterize Piero's style

---

the city into one of the most advanced cultural centers of the day. The paintings Piero made in Urbino include a small picture of the flagellation of Christ (1450s), a pair of portraits of Federico and his second wife Battista Sforza (after 1465), and *The Brera Altarpiece* (1472–1474), an imposing picture of the Madonna and Child (Mary and Jesus), with saints and the kneeling figure of Federico set in a carefully detailed classical building.

The Flagellation of Christ sums up Piero's style. It shows the moment mentioned in the Bible when Pontius Pilate (shown seated on the throne) instructed soldiers to flog Christ before

he is crucified. Piero depicted the scene in an unusual way, showing the flagellation taking place in the background of the left half of the picture, while three unidentified figures on the right dominate the painting. The picture is an advanced exercise in perspective, or the depiction of figures in space, and Piero used a very precise system to show how the floor tiles and lines of the ceiling appear to recede. The clear outlines, bright lighting, pure colors, and sense of stillness characterize Piero's style.

WRITING ABOUT ART AND MATH

In the 1470s and 1480s Piero devoted himself increasingly to writing about mathematics. He wrote an influential treatise (book) about perspective and two about applied mathematics. These works reflect the influence of Alberti and were to inspire younger artists like Leonardo da Vinci. After Piero's death in 1492 his clear, ordered painting style lived on in the work of Perugino—a painter most scholars believe was one of Piero's pupils—and Perugino in turn passed on his harmonious style and poetic sense of space to his greatest pupil: Raphael.

Above: Piero della Francesca's **The Flagellation of Christ** *(late 1450s). The painting has a still, mysterious air resulting from the complex system of perspective Piero used to create a feeling of space. The picture is like a mathematical puzzle and has long fascinated scholars.*

SEE ALSO

♦ Alberti
♦ Angelico, Fra
♦ Donatello
♦ Leonardo da Vinci
♦ Naturalism
♦ Painting
♦ Perspective
♦ Raphael
♦ Theories of Art and Architecture
♦ Urbino

Plague and Disease

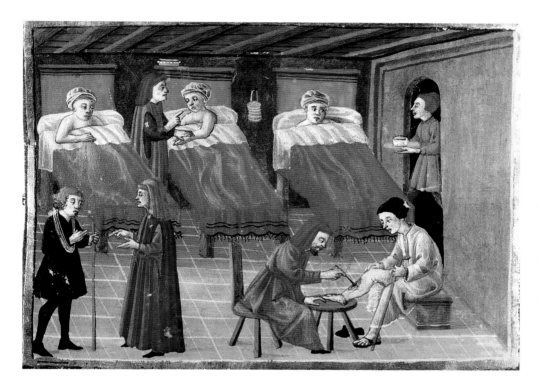

Left: This illustration from a 15th-century manuscript shows the daily routine in an Italian hospital. In many hospitals monks and nuns cared for the dying, providing them with simple medical help. Wealthier sufferers hired trained doctors, but doctors were unable to cure diseases such as the plague.

From the 14th century many people in Europe died from a series of epidemics (fast-spreading diseases). Trade, war, and dirty living conditions in the flourishing cities of Renaissance Europe encouraged these epidemics. The most serious was the Black Death (also called the plague), which killed a third of Europe's population in the late 1340s. The deadly diseases typhus and syphilis also became widespread during the course of the 16th century, and a dangerous strain of influenza struck western Europe in the 1550s.

The Black Death reached Italy from Central Asia in 1348 and spread rapidly through Europe, reaching England and Germany in less than a year. It was a devastating mixture of two related diseases: bubonic plague and pneumonic plague. The bubonic form is carried by fleas living on black rats, while pneumonic plague is airborne, fast-spreading, and lethal. The more common bubonic form caused boil-like swellings (buboes) in the victim's groin area and armpits. After three or four days of fever, vomiting, and delirium (a confused, nightmarelike state) the victim usually died.

There were four further outbreaks of the plague during the 14th century, and another at the end of the 15th century, in which many regions of Europe lost half their populations.

Local authorities established public health measures in the wake of the Black Death, keeping records of plague

SMALLPOX CONQUERS THE NEW WORLD

One consequence of the European discovery of America was the spread of diseases such as smallpox, measles, and typhus to the New World. The symptoms of smallpox were fever and pus-filled swellings on the victim's face, hands, and feet, which left the survivors scarred for life. It spread so rapidly among the Mexican Aztecs, who had no natural immunity (resistance) to these new diseases, that when Spaniards entered the Aztec capital in 1521, they found half the population dead. Ten years later the same pattern was repeated among the Incas of Peru. While the disease left the Spaniards untouched, it killed thousands of Aztecs and Incas, so helping the Spanish to conquer the Americas.

deaths and isolating the sick from the healthy. Mediterranean ports imposed quarantines. This involved preventing ships suspected of carrying diseases from docking for 40 days, but the rats still managed to reach the shore. Measures to tackle the disease were not very effective because people did not understand how the disease was transmitted; unsanitary (dirty) and overcrowded dwellings in towns created ideal breeding conditions for plague-carrying rats. It was not until the 18th century that improved sanitation drove the plague away.

Even though physicians could not cure the plague, people still turned to them for help. Treatments ranged from opening the buboes with a razor and applying blood-sucking leeches to burning the buboes, then covering the wound with cabbage leaves.

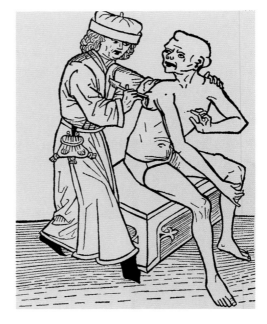

Left: This German woodcut from 1482 shows a doctor lancing (cutting open) a boil to draw out the pus. Boils that swelled up under the arms were symptoms of bubonic plague. This form of the plague was carried by fleas and could not be caught from another person.

TYPHUS AND SYPHILIS

The symptoms of typhus were as horrible as those of the plague; they included fever, gangrene (as fingers and toes rotted away), and delirium. Typhus was introduced to Europe from Asia during conflicts between Christians and Muslims in the late 15th and mid-16th century, and it killed far more soldiers than ever killed each other. Typhus spread rapidly in army camps and prisons, where men lived in crowded, dirty conditions. Unwashed clothes encouraged the body lice that carried the typhus bacteria.

Syphilis appeared around the same time, at the French siege of Naples in 1494, before being spread across Europe by mercenary soldiers who had been fighting for the French. A sexually transmitted disease, syphilis was a slow killer with spreading sores and ulcers that rotted the skin and made the hair fall out. By 1600 it had been carried around the world by European soldiers and sailors involved in European expansion and exploration.

SEE ALSO
♦ Americas
♦ Anatomy
♦ Children
♦ Houses
♦ London
♦ Medicine and Surgery
♦ Population
♦ Poverty
♦ Towns
♦ Trade

Poetry

The poets of the Renaissance reflected the spirit of their age. As well as being interested in the writers and poets of antiquity, they also aimed to tell entertaining stories that would be read and enjoyed by educated lay (nonchurch) people rather than scholars and churchmen. So, many of them wrote their poems in their native (vernacular) language rather than Latin.

Like all other writers of the time, poets were influenced by the ideas of humanism and the revival of interest in the classical (ancient Greek and Roman) world. They enjoyed writing in some of the classical forms, such as the epic, the pastoral, and the satire. But instead of following strict rules of style or language, they concentrated on the free play of the imagination, the love of storytelling, and the description of mood or emotion that they found in their classical models.

In the late 13th century the Italian poet Dante (1265–1321) published his *Vita nuova* ("The New Life"), a set of 31 love poems written in the Italian language. From that time Italian became the leading literary language of Europe, and Italian literature became a hotbed of new ideas and experimental techniques. Poetry took off in two directions—long verse romances and epic poems based on classical models, and short poems focusing on the experience and feelings of one individual.

Dante's younger contemporary Petrarch (1304–1374) was devoted to the revival of classical learning and

Right: A 15th-century fresco of the Italian poet Dante. He wrote poems in Italian, starting the fashion for poets to write in their own language rather than Latin.

THE SONNET

The sonnet was developed in the 13th century by court poets in Sicily. In the 14th century it became a hugely successful and influential poetic form in the hands of Petrarch. A sonnet always has 14 lines. Petrarch established a particular form of sonnet, which became known as the Italian sonnet. The opening eight lines, known as the "octave," pose a problem or a question, or describe some difficulty that needs resolution. These lines rhyme abbaabba. The last six lines, the "sestet," contain a twist or a new point of view that answers the question or resolves the problem. The sestet can have either two or three new rhyme-words in varying sequences.

The sonnet form is perfectly suited to the elegant expression of feelings, especially romantic feelings. Petrarch also established a new way of using sonnets, which was to write lots of them in sequence to tell a story. This innovation was possibly the single most influential development in Renaissance poetry—the sonnet sequence was adored and imitated in Italy, and soon spread to every other European country, where it was adapted to suit the local language.

The sonnet reached England in the mid-16th century and triggered an explosion of Elizabethan lyric poetry (a lyric poem is a short poem that expresses the poet's own thoughts and feelings). English poets invented their own particular form of the sonnet. It consisted of three quatrains (four lines of verse), which developed the main ideas and images of the poem, followed by a brilliant, witty rhyming couplet (two lines of verse) at the end.

English poets loved to write sonnet sequences. Although each sonnet in the sequence could stand alone, together they told a story that related the course of a love affair. Sir Philip Sidney's sonnet sequence *Astrophel and Stella* (1580–1584) told the story of his idealized love for Lady Penelope Rich, and Edmund Spenser's *Amoretti* (1591) celebrated his love for Elizabeth Boyle, whom he later married. Shakespeare's sonnets were different from others of the time. Rather than telling a story, they meditated on all kinds of things—the changeability of the human heart, the short life of beauty, and the power of poetry to confer immortality on its subject.

Right: A 15th-century illustration for the first French edition of the Decameron ("Ten Days") by the Italian poet Boccaccio. The stories in the Decameron were to be the inspiration for many works by later poets.

language. However, he also wrote a collection of love lyrics and sonnets in Italian called the *Canzoniere* in praise of Laura, a married lady whom he worshiped from afar for 16 years. The sonnet sequence was very influential and was much imitated by his successors in Italy and throughout Europe.

A LITERARY GIANT

Another literary giant of 14th-century Italy was Boccaccio (1313–1375), whose stories in verse form were extremely popular and influential. His *Il Filostrato,* for instance, told the ancient story of Troilus and Cressida, lovers during the Trojan War. It was to inspire the English poet Geoffrey Chaucer (about 1342–1400) to write a poem on the same subject and later formed the basis for Shakespeare's play

Troilus and Cressida. Boccaccio combined a respect for classical forms with his own irreverent humor and uninhibited realism. His collection of tales in prose, the *Decameron* ("Ten Days"), inspired Chaucer to write his *Canterbury Tales* and influenced many later Italian poets.

France in the 15th century saw the brief career of François Villon (1431–after 1463), who managed to write great lyric poems while leading a wild, hard-drinking, violent life. Villon's poems are remarkable for their powerful emotional energy and their tough realism in evoking the taverns,

Left: A 16th-century portrait of Ludovico Ariosto, the Italian poet who wrote the romantic epic **Orlando Furioso.** *The poem had a pastoral theme and helped make the pastoral romance a popular form.*

> ## *Villon's poems are remarkable for their powerful emotional energy and tough realism*

brothels, and prisons of 15th-century Paris. His major poems, *Le Petit Testament* ("The Little Testament"), *Le Grand Testament* ("The Great Testament"), and *Le Ballade des Pendus* ("The Ballad of the Hanged Men"), remain personal and piercing for modern readers.

The late 15th century saw the revival of a form of narrative poem popular in classical Greece—the pastoral—which told tales of an idealized life in the countryside. One of the greatest writers of the new pastoral romance was the Italian Ludovico Ariosto (1474–1533),

ORLANDO FURIOSO

Orlando Furioso was supposed to be an epic poem (a poem dealing with heroic themes), but it is very different from the classical epics of Virgil and Homer. It does not celebrate heroic deeds or show the hero fighting against overwhelming odds. Instead, it tells the story of Orlando, who has become temporarily insane because of his unrequited love for the beautiful Angelica, an Indian princess. Orlando charges around the countryside, out of his mind with pain and grief, while his friends attempt to restore his sanity. One manages to travel to the moon, which is the repository for everything that has been lost on earth. Here he finds things such as wasted time and money, broken vows, bellows for inflating empty promises, and the pride of fallen kingdoms. The one thing he does not find is any folly—it is all still on earth. The voice of the narrator is detached and seems disillusioned with human hopes and passions. The reader's interest is sustained by the interplay of the characters, the exploration of their feelings and strivings, their romantic longing for a better life, and the sense of the fragility of everything they hold dear.

whose *Orlando Furioso* ("Roland Deranged") was a huge success and was translated and imitated throughout Europe (see box on page 33). It ushered in a new type of literature in which the realism and earthly passions of Villon gave way to romantic fantasies written in hauntingly beautiful verse and full of aristocratic longings for the simple pastoral life. *Orlando* inspired Sir Philip Sidney's prose fantasy *Arcadia* and Edmund Spenser's delicate verse masterpiece *The Faerie Queene*.

AN ITALIAN MASTERPIECE

The late 16th century produced one more great poet from Italy—Torquato Tasso (1544–1595). Tasso's masterpiece, *Gerusalemme liberata* ("Jerusalem Delivered"), tells the story of the final few months of the First Crusade in 1099, when the Christian forces reconquered Jerusalem and founded four Christian states in Palestine. Tasso transformed the bare historical facts into an exuberant and powerful romance. He added the story of the Italian hero Rinaldo and his love for the Saracen maiden Armida, and reinvented the character of the historical Tancred de Hauteville as a romantic young hero in love with the beautiful Saracen warrior princess Clorinda. One of the great moments in the poem is when Tancred meets Clorinda in battle without knowing who she is and mortally wounds her. Before she dies in his arms, the two declare their love, and Clorinda is converted to Christianity. Because of its emotional depth and martial vigor the poem seems more like an epic than a romance.

Above: A 19th-century painting of the poet Tasso reading his work to the ladies of the court at Ferrara, where the duke was his patron.

SEE ALSO

♦ Boccaccio
♦ Chaucer
♦ Chivalry
♦ Christine de Pisan
♦ Dante
♦ Language
♦ Literature
♦ Petrarch
♦ Shakespeare

Population

Above: A detail from a 15th-century fresco (wall painting) showing villagers harvesting wheat. A great number of harvests failed in the 14th century, causing famines in which many people died.

In the 14th century Europe was struck by two calamities—famine and the plague. It is thought that of the 75 million people living in Europe at that time, about one-third, or 25 million, of them died. The 15th and 16th centuries, on the other hand, saw a slow and steady rise in population—between 1400 and 1600 the population of Europe grew from about 50 million to 80 million.

At the beginning of the 14th century famine may have been responsible for almost as many deaths as the plague. There was a series of disastrous crop failures—about one every five years—which meant that many people died of hunger. Constant hunger also meant that those who remained alive had less resistance to disease. The plague arrived in Europe in 1348, probably carried by rats and fleas on ships from the Crimea. It spread with frightening speed throughout Europe, reaching Scotland and Scandinavia by December 1349. This widespread outbreak was known as the Black Death; once someone contracted the disease, it was almost certain they would die. The plague had a devastating effect on the population, and less ferocious outbreaks continued to flare up all over Europe for the next 300 years.

FEWER TO FEED

This dramatic reduction in the number of people had several results. Because there were fewer people to feed, less land was needed to grow crops. People stopped trying to farm the less fertile areas, and small villages on unproductive land were abandoned in favor of larger villages on better farming land. Although less food was produced following the plague, prices began to fall because there were fewer people to buy it. Agriculture became more varied as farmers began to turn to more profitable stockbreeding and sheep-rearing. Cereal crops began to be imported from the arable lands of eastern Europe, where the effect of the plague had not been so severe. Since there was now more food for those who had survived, there was a gradual rise in population throughout Europe in the late 15th and early 16th centuries.

In the postplague years people approached marriage and childbearing with caution. The average age of marriage in northern and western Europe was fairly high—most women did not marry until they were about 25 years old, and men tended to be older still. In south and southeastern Europe

Left: A painting entitled A Country Wedding *by Pieter Bruegel the Elder (about 1525–1569). Village weddings were occasions for feasting and merry-making. The happy couple could expect to have six children, but it was doubtful whether they would live long enough to see them grow up.*

people tended to marry at a slightly earlier age. In northern and western Europe about half the people of marriageable age were single—many of these single people were monks and nuns. Women who married at 25 could expect a childbearing period of about 15 years. Births in general were spaced at intervals of approximately 30 months, so that the average family had six children. Child mortality, however, was very high. Up to a third of all children died in their first year; only half of them, on average, survived to the age of 10.

A SHORT LIFE

The average age to which people could expect to live was very low throughout Europe—about 35 years. People died young for a number of reasons. Many women died in childbirth. People suffered from malnutrition when food was short, as it often was in late winter, and this meant they were more vulnerable to diseases such as plague, tuberculosis, and typhus. People did not understand that insanitary conditions helped these infections spread, and that made the problem worse.

Warfare also meant that people might die young. These were violent

---

The savage wars of religion in the 16th century killed many people

---

times. There was continuous conflict in France, the Rhineland, and Italy in the late 15th century, and the savage wars of religion in the 16th century killed many people. In addition, terrible devastation was inflicted on both people and property by roving bands of mercenaries, professional soldiers who would fight for the highest bidder. Warfare not only claimed many lives, it also created uncertain conditions that did not encourage settled family life and a rising birthrate.

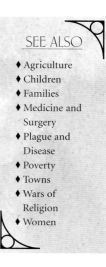

SEE ALSO

- Agriculture
- Children
- Families
- Medicine and Surgery
- Plague and Disease
- Poverty
- Towns
- Wars of Religion
- Women

Portraiture

A portrait is a likeness of a person, particularly their face. The Renaissance was an important period in the development of portraiture because it was the first time since antiquity (ancient Greece and Rome) that portraits became an art form in their own right. From the 15th century important individuals commissioned pictures and sculptures of themselves to display and record their wealth and power.

In the 15th century humanism, a new type of learning based on the study of ancient Greek and Roman texts, created an environment in which portraiture could flourish. Unlike medieval ways of thinking, humanism placed a new emphasis on the role of the individual. One result of this development was that patrons (people who paid for art) began to order paintings and sculptures of themselves. These patrons included not only members of royalty, the nobility, and the church, but also self-made men: powerful mercenary soldiers, bankers, and merchants.

The revived interest in classical (ancient Greek and Roman) culture also had a direct effect on artistic approaches and values. Painters and sculptors of the 15th century studied sculptures that survived from ancient times—virtually no paintings were known—and copied what they saw. In general, classical sculpture was much more naturalistic, or lifelike, than medieval art, which was often stylized (artificial looking) and symbolic. As

Renaissance artists sought to achieve similar effects, they became more skilled in the naturalistic portrayal of the world around them.

The sculptures that survived from ancient Rome included several types of portrait, among them marble busts (sculptures of the head and shoulders of a person) and a few large equestrian statues that showed rulers on horseback. Both these types of sculpture were commemorative. Busts were used by important families to record their ancestors, while equestrian statues celebrated the achievements of great

Above: **Portrait of a Young Man with a Medal of Cosimo de Medici,** *painted in about 1474 by Sandro Botticelli. The picture is two portraits in one. Scholars think the young man could be Cosimo's son Piero, the artist who made the medal, or a loyal supporter of the Medici family.*

SCULPTED PORTRAITS

During the 15th century carved portrait busts became popular in Florence. They were based on ancient Roman portrait busts—indeed, Renaissance sculptors often showed their sitters wearing Roman togas rather than 15th-century clothes—and, like them, were very lifelike. Most surviving Renaissance busts show men, though a few show women and children, and their names are carved on the base or back of the sculpture. They were intended to ensure that the fame of these wealthy individuals lived on after their death. Portrait busts were usually displayed inside the home, although they were sometimes placed on the outside of buildings, above the door, for example. Some of the greatest portrait busts were carved by the sculptors Mino da Fiesole, Antonio Rossellino, Benedetto da Maiano, and Andrea Verrocchio.

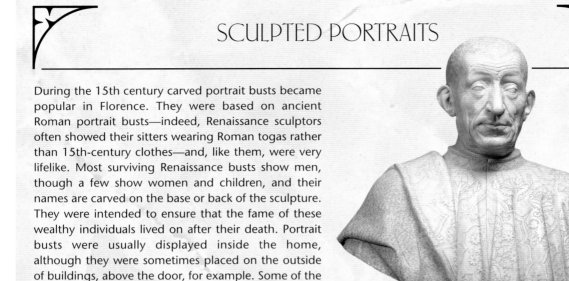

Above: A bust of Pietro Mellini by Benedetto da Maiano (1474). Mellini was a wealthy merchant.

emperors or leaders. Classical coins also had accurate portraits on the front. The portraits were profiles (showing the face viewed from the side), and there were inscriptions that identified the person shown.

THE DEVELOPMENT OF PORTRAITS

These coins had a great influence on Renaissance portraiture. They appealed to powerful rulers because they offered a way of ensuring that their fame lived on even after death. Some of the first realistic portraits made in 15th-century Italy took the form of medals based on antique coins. Andrea Pisanello (about 1395–1455) was the first Renaissance artist to design medals, and he produced them for many Italian courts. They were large and impressive, usually made from bronze, and had accurate profile portraits and inscriptions.

Pisanello was also a painter, and he portrayed people in the same way in his painted portraits—that is, he showed the head and shoulders of the sitter

(person portrayed) in profile. Many other artists, including Botticelli and Piero della Francesca, adopted this format for their portraits. However, it was a rather rigid and unnatural way to depict people, and from the 1470s artists produced portraits that showed the whole of the sitter's face.

Often artists showed more than just the head and shoulders of the sitter. Sometimes they depicted the body down to the waist (a three-quarter-length portrait) or sometimes the whole body (a full-length portrait). On some occasions powerful leaders or soldiers were portrayed sitting on horseback in reference to classical equestrian monuments—*Charles V after the Battle of Mühlberg* (1548), by the 16th-century Venetian painter Titian, is the best-known example of this type of painting. The number of people shown in portraits also varied. It might be one person, a husband and wife, a family, or an entire household, as in Andrea Mantegna's frescoes (wall paintings) in the ducal palace at Mantua (about 1474), painted to glorify the Gonzaga court.

THE FUNCTION OF PORTRAITS

The primary function of most portraits was to display the status, or the power and wealth, of the person shown. This aim was achieved not only by referring back to classical models, but also by showing the sitter wearing expensive clothes and jewelry and set in lavish surroundings. In some cases rulers were depicted in front of a landscape that showed the territories they ruled over. People were also portrayed with objects that related to their profession, family, interests, or personal qualities. For example, soldiers were depicted in armor with their weapons, churchmen in official robes, and scholars were shown reading or writing in a study.

Other portraits were painted for more private, intimate purposes, to show a loved one—a wife or child, for example. In France and England during the 16th century small portraits of this type, called miniatures, became very popular. They were often worn in lockets and served as mementoes.

Left: Titian's painting Charles V after the Battle of Mühlberg *(1548). The picture celebrates the Holy Roman emperor's victory over Protestant princes at the battle of Mühlberg. Titian drew on the tradition of ancient Roman equestrian sculptures and created a powerful image of Charles dressed in armor, holding a lance, and sitting astride a charging steed.*

Many of the leading Italian artists of the Renaissance painted portraits—Giovanni Bellini, Raphael, and Titian in particular excelled in the art form—and so too did painters working in northern Europe, in Flanders (a region that includes present-day Belgium and parts of the Netherlands and France), and in Germany.

NORTHERN EUROPEAN PORTRAITS

Northern European portraits tend to be extremely lifelike, showing every wrinkle, hair, and detail of the sitter. The Flemish artist Jan van Eyck painted some of the best-known portraits of the period, including *Portrait of Cardinal Albergati* (1432) and *The Arnolfini Marriage* (1434, see Volume 4, page 4). Van Eyck developed the use of oil paint to help him create detailed pictures with subtle effects of color and tone (light and shade). Oil paint is slow-drying, which enables artists to spend time painting details, and can be applied in thin, transparent layers to build up color and tone. Van Eyck's paintings influenced artists in Italy and Germany as well as Flanders.

In Germany they were admired by Albrecht Dürer (1471–1528), who himself produced detailed portrait

Left: Jan van Eyck's Portrait of Cardinal Albergati (about 1432). Van Eyck painted remarkably lifelike, vivid portraits that recorded every detail of his sitter's appearance. His paintings were very popular with patrons and influenced artists in both northern Europe and Italy.

drawings and paintings, including several self-portraits. Self-portraits became common in the Renaissance as artists drew and painted themselves for practice or, like their patrons, to emphasize their increasing status. Another great artist from Germany, Hans Holbein (1497–1543), specialized in portrait painting, and his pictures of kings, scholars, merchants, and ambassadors combine the grandeur of Italian painting with the realistic, detailed style of northern Europe.

DONOR PORTRAITS

From the 15th century portraits were increasingly included in paintings and stained glass windows with religious subjects like the Madonna and Child (Mary and Jesus). These portraits are called "donor portraits" because they show the people who paid for the picture or window and gave ("donated") it to the church. The donors are usually shown kneeling at the sides of the picture and are smaller in size than the holy figures. Donor figures were included in many religious paintings throughout the Renaissance: Masaccio's *The Holy Trinity* (about 1425), Piero della Francesca's *Brera Altarpiece* (1470s), and Hugo van der Goes' *Portinari Altarpiece* (1475) are well-known examples.

Portugal

Portugal is a small country on the western edge of the Spanish peninsula. During the Middle Ages it had been a poor country with few resources apart from wine, salt, and the fish of the Atlantic Ocean. But the 15th and 16th centuries were to be Portugal's golden age. Daring feats of exploration took Portuguese seafarers around Africa and on to India, with momentous consequences. For a time the small country grew wealthy from trade with the East and became the center of a great colonial empire.

Much of Portugal's earlier history had been concerned with struggles between its kings and groups of powerful nobles, complicated by disputes with Portugal's much stronger neighbor, Castile (which in 1479 became part of the kingdom of Spain). These conflicts continued in the 15th century, but there were important new developments. An expansive Portuguese spirit began to show itself under King John I

(ruled 1385–1433), the founder of the Avis dynasty (see box). In 1415 a Portuguese expedition conquered the Muslim stronghold of Ceuta in Morocco on the North African coast. Portugal made further attempts to expand in North Africa with mixed results, but the real importance of the episode was its effect on Prince Henry,

Above: Prince Henry (holding the map)—known as the Navigator—with his captains at the school of navigation he founded in Sagres, Portugal.

 A NEW DYNASTY

When Ferdinand I of Portugal died in 1383, his heir was his daughter Beatrice, who had married King John of Castile. Many Portuguese nobles and churchmen were willing to accept John and Beatrice as monarchs, but the people were opposed to rule by Castilians. After a period of turmoil Ferdinand's illegitimate half-brother, John of Avis, was appointed regent of the kingdom. The Castilians tried to assert their claim by besieging Lisbon, but were driven off by an outbreak of plague. Then in April 1385 the Portuguese Cortes elected John of Avis king, as John I. When the Castilians again invaded in August, they were crushed at the battle of Aljubarrota. Archers from a friendly England fought in the battle, and in 1386 Portugal and England signed an "eternal" alliance, which did in fact last for hundreds of years. John became the founder of the Avis dynasty, and his children included two kings and Prince Henry the Navigator.

Right: A map of Portugal and the Spanish peninsula in the mid-15th century. Lisbon became the center of a huge trading empire after Vasco da Gama reached India in 1498.

the coast of Africa as far as present-day Sierra Leone. By the 1460s the Portuguese were making profits from gold and the trade in African slaves.

Henry is now remembered as "Henry the Navigator" because he founded a school of navigation at Sagres—he didn't actually sail on any of the voyages he planned. After his death little more exploration was done until King John II (ruled 1481–1491) strengthened royal power at home. He sent expeditions east by land to India and Abyssinia and south by sea into the Atlantic again. The Portuguese were now seeking spices, pepper, cotton, and other Asian products, which would be obtainable if they could find a sea route to the East. In 1488 Bartholomeu Dias succeeded in rounding the Cape of Good Hope, Africa's southern tip, and 10 years later, under King Manuel I (ruled 1495–1521), Vasco da Gama reached India.

the king's third son. At Ceuta he learned of caravans (groups of people traveling with animals to carry their goods) that transported gold across the Sahara Desert from West Africa. He resolved to find a way of reaching this source of fabulous wealth.

PORTUGUESE EXPLORATION

From 1416 until his death in 1460 Henry sent out expeditions to explore the west coast of Africa. Successive expeditions discovered two groups of uninhabited islands in the Atlantic Ocean—the Madeiras and Azores—and gradually worked their way down

WEALTH AND EXPANSION

Da Gama's return to Portugal with a cargo of Asian goods began an economic revolution. Although prices of eastern commodities fell sharply in

THE NATIONAL EPIC

The Portuguese nation and its achievements were honored in a famous epic poem entitled *The Lusiads*, which was a poetic name for the Portuguese people. Its author, Luis de Camões, was born around 1524, probably in Lisbon. Though he spent some time at the royal court, an unhappy love affair led him to enlist as a soldier. He was posted to Ceuta in North Africa, where he lost an eye in battle before returning to Portugal in 1549. After being involved in a street fight, he

was briefly imprisoned and then, in 1553, sent to India. Work and travel took him to Macao on the Chinese coast, the Spice Islands (in present-day Indonesia), and Mozambique in Africa. After 17 years he returned to Lisbon and published his great poem, whose central episodes describe Vasco da Gama's epoch-making voyage to India. During his lifetime Camões received only limited recognition in the form of a small pension, and he died a poor man in 1580.

Europe, there were still huge profits to be made, and Lisbon, the Portuguese capital, became Europe's principal marketplace. Wealth flowed into the country, and a period of lavish building began. A new highly decorative style of architecture developed called the Manueline (after Manuel I). Literature and the arts flourished, producing the playwrights Sá de Miranda and Gil Vicente, the poet Luis de Camões (see box), and the painter Nuño Gonçalves.

THE TREATY OF TORDESILLAS

In 1494 Portugal and Spain had signed the Treaty of Tordesillas, which divided the newly discovered lands between them. A north–south line, drawn down the globe 370 leagues (about 1,100 miles/1,760km) west of the Cape Verde Islands, gave all lands to the west to Spain and lands to the east to Portugal.

This meant that most of the Americas went to Spain, while the Portuguese received Brazil (discovered in 1500), Africa, and the East. Since America's potential had not yet been recognized, Portugal seemed to have benefited the most once da Gama reached India.

Portugal became even stronger as able viceroys, appointed to run the country's overseas affairs, established new bases and pushed eastward as far as China and Japan. They founded a new kind of empire based on commerce rather than conquest, establishing trading posts and forts along the African coast, on the Persian Gulf, at Cochin and Goa in India, and at points even further east, including Melaka, Macao, and Nagasaki.

In 1557 John III died, and his three-year-old grandson Sebastian became king. Sebastian's education filled him

Below: A 16th-century tapestry showing Vasco da Gama landing at Calicut in southern India. Da Gama was the first European explorer to find an eastward sea route to India. He left Lisbon in July 1497 and reached Calicut in May 1498.

with visions of leading a crusade against Islam; and when he came of age, he rashly decided to attack Morocco in North Africa. In June 1578 he led 15,000 infantry and 1,500 cavalry into action at Alcacer Quibir. The battle was a disaster for the Portuguese army, which was utterly

King Philip II of Spain promised to rule Portugal through Portuguese officials and to uphold national rights and customs

destroyed. Sebastian himself was killed. However, his body was never found, and for years after pretenders appeared claiming to be the missing king. Sebastian had no children, and he was succeeded by his great-uncle, the aged Cardinal Henry. When Henry died in 1580, the situation was confused, and there were a number of claimants to the throne.

SPANISH RULE

The claimants included King Philip II of Spain, the most powerful monarch in Europe, who was a grandson of Portugal's King Manuel I. After the long history of Portuguese–Spanish conflict many Portuguese were reluctant to accept him, but Philip ensured his success by sending an army into Portugal. In 1581 the Cortes—the national assembly of nobles, clergy, and commons—hailed him as king.

Philip promised to rule through Portuguese officials and uphold national rights and customs, and on the whole he kept his promise. But Portugal was drawn into Spain's wars

with the Dutch and the English, with the result that the country suffered economically and also lost some of its best warships when they took part in the disastrous Armada sent by Spain against England in 1588.

After Philip's death in 1598 Spanish rule became more oppressive. In 1640, taking advantage of a time when Spain was in difficulties, the Portuguese rebelled and broke away, choosing a king of their own. However, by this time they had lost their great naval and trading power to the Dutch. Portugal had regained its independence, but the golden age was over.

Above: A street in Goa, India. The city became the capital of the Portuguese Empire in the East.

SEE ALSO

- Africa
- Exploration
- Literature
- Navigation
- Philip II
- Ships
- Spain
- Trade

Poverty

Left: A detail from
The Struggle
between Carnival
and Lent, *by Pieter*
Bruegel the Elder
(about 1525–1569).
The painting shows
a group of poor and
crippled people
begging for money
from a prosperous
citizen. The gulf
between rich and
poor in the
Renaissance
period was huge.

The lives of the poor in Renaissance times were grim. People who lost their homes and their jobs usually became beggars, wandering the countryside or drifting to the towns. Once someone had sunk this far, there was little hope that things would ever improve for them.

There were various reasons why people became destitute (without food or shelter). Men and women might leave their village when famine struck, or when low wages and rising prices made it impossible for them to support themselves. If a man was married, and particularly if he had children, he might take to the road in search of better paid work, leaving his wife and children behind. If a working man

died, his widow was generally left without adequate means. Even if she had a skill of her own, such as lacemaking, she would be unable to earn enough to feed herself and her children. Other destitute people were the old, who could no longer work, and children who were orphans or who had been abandoned by their parents.

The authorities tried to help the poor of their own parish. Alms (money for charitable relief) were handed out in churches and city halls, and in the towns there were poorhouses and foundling hospitals for orphans. But there was never enough charity to help the wandering bands of beggars, many of whom turned to crime.

Even when poor people managed to remain at work, their lives were a constant struggle. Their diet was inadequate, consisting mainly of cereals and beans or lentils. This led to health problems such as lameness, blindness, deafness, and tooth decay. There were regular outbreaks of diseases such as bubonic plague, smallpox, typhus, and tuberculosis, to which the poor were specially vulnerable because of their unclean living conditions. People died young. One-third of infants died in their first year, and many mothers died in childbirth, partly due to the unsanitary conditions in which they lived.

Left: A 15th-century stained-glass window in a church in York, England, showing bread being distributed to the poor. Each parish tried to look after its own poor, but there was never enough money to help everyone.

MISERABLE WINTERS

Winter was a disastrous time. There was little to eat, and living conditions were primitive. Most houses of the poor, in town and country alike, were small two-roomed structures, poorly lighted, drafty, and with unglazed windows. The only source of heat was a fire—but it often filled the house with acrid smoke, and the choice was to shiver or to choke. The houses smelled bad inside because there was no good way of disposing of sewage, and animals often lived under the same roof. Clean, fresh water was difficult to obtain; people rarely washed themselves or their clothes, and body odors must have been overpowering.

Poor people had very little leisure. Their lives were dominated by hard work from dawn to dusk. Any entertainments they had were provided by festivals and carnivals. Those who had a little money to spare might spend it in the tavern or at the theater.

LONDON'S POOR

England's capital city, London, was much smaller in the 16th century than it is today, yet it acted as a magnet for poor people from all over the country. When they reached the city, however, these country folk found overcrowded conditions, filthy streets, and a contaminated water supply. The death rate in some London parishes was much higher than anywhere else in the country. In the poorest parishes people could not expect to live beyond 20 to 25 years. Yet even the plague, which in 1563 killed nearly a quarter of the city's population, failed to check London's growth. In 1580 Queen Elizabeth I issued a proclamation on the living conditions of the poor in London, pointing out that "great multitudes of people [are] brought to inhabit in small rooms . . . heaped up together, and in a sort smothered with many families of children and servants in one house or small tenement." As a result, it was decreed that only one family should inhabit each house. Although impossible to enforce, this decree was the first attempt to enact a law that would improve the living conditions of London's poor.

Printing

The invention of printing with movable type and a specially designed press was one of the most influential developments to take place in Europe during the Renaissance period. It meant that books could be produced far more quickly and cheaply than the handwritten manuscripts of the Middle Ages. Now that people could afford to buy books, new ideas spread rapidly.

In the Middle Ages manuscripts and books were extremely rare and valuable items. They were hand-written on parchment or vellum, expensive materials made from prepared animal skins, and were decorated with painted designs and gold. Most books were made in monasteries by scribes working in workshops called scriptoria. Monasteries also owned the only libraries of the time.

However, from about the 12th century, when towns began to gain in importance and the first universities grew up, nonreligious bookmakers and booksellers began to set up workshops in prosperous cities like Paris. As demand for texts increased from scholars and wealthy educated people, it became increasingly desirable to discover a more rapid and efficient means of producing books.

EARLY PRINTED BOOKS

Around the end of the 14th century and the beginning of the 15th century European craftsmen began to make prints called woodcuts using wooden blocks carved with designs. They were usually pictures of religious subjects like Bible stories, the Madonna and

Above: A 17th-century engraving of a printing shop—a scene that would have changed little since the Renaissance. In the foreground men remove printed pages from presses. In the background they can be seen arranging pieces of type in wooden frames for printing.

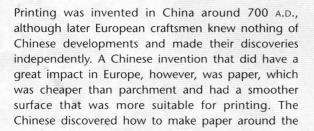

CHINESE DEVELOPMENTS

Printing was invented in China around 700 A.D., although later European craftsmen knew nothing of Chinese developments and made their discoveries independently. A Chinese invention that did have a great impact in Europe, however, was paper, which was cheaper than parchment and had a smoother surface that was more suitable for printing. The Chinese discovered how to make paper around the first century A.D., but their methods remained a closely guarded secret until the eighth century, when a group of Chinese craftsmen was taken prisoner by Arabs. Papermaking skills then spread rapidly through the Islamic Empire and reached Europe by the 12th century. Paper mills were established in Spain and Italy around 1150, in France in 1189, in Germany in 1320, and in England in 1494.

Child (Mary and Jesus), and scenes from the saints' lives. As craftsmen became increasingly skilled at carving, they also included text in their designs; and in the first half of the 15th century printed pages were bound together to produce books called "blockbooks."

Woodcuts produced quite crude prints, and each page of text had to be carved afresh. From around 1430 skilled metalworkers experimented with making dies (metal molds with an engraved design) for each character required—letters, numbers, and punctuation marks. These dies were used to punch the design for a page of text onto a clay mold, onto which molten lead was then poured. The resulting lead sheet was used to print from. Lead was more durable than wood, and the system of using a single die for each letter ensured that all the letters printed from that die looked the same.

JOHANNES GUTENBERG

However, the greatest advances in printing were made around 1450 with the invention of movable type and the printing press in Germany. Most scholars attribute these important inventions to the German silversmith Johannes Gutenberg (about 1390s–1468), although the descendants of his business partners disputed his role.

With movable type each character, or piece of "type," is a separate block and can be reused. Each piece of type is made by pouring an alloy—a mixture of lead, tin, and antimony—into a die that has been carved with a character.

A page of text is made by arranging the pieces of type to form words and sentences and then locking them together in a frame called a "form." After printing, the type can be taken out of the form, ready to be used again. Gutenberg placed type set in a form on a printing press, the design of which was based on machines used to press grapes for wine. The press consisted of a fixed lower surface (the bed) and a movable upper surface (the platen), which could be lowered or raised by turning a large screw. Type was placed on the bed, then inked, and a piece of paper was put on top. The screw was then turned to press the platen onto the paper. Applying pressure in this way produced a sharp and even print. Gutenberg used his new inventions to print his own edition of the Bible, which was published in three volumes in 1456. It is the earliest book produced with movable type.

Printing spread quickly throughout Europe, and presses had been set up in both Paris and Venice by 1470. It was

Below: A modern reconstruction of Gutenberg's printing workshop in the German city of Mainz.

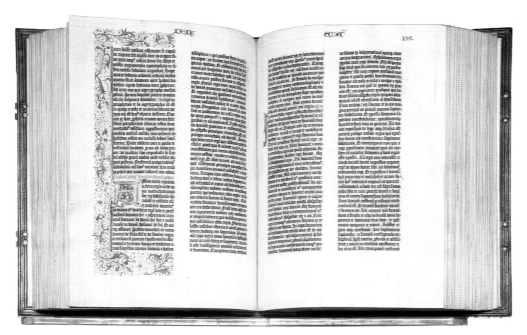

Left: Gutenberg's Bible (1456), which is also known as the "Forty-two-Line Bible" because each column has 42 lines of text. It looks similar to earlier handwritten books and was printed using Gothic type, which was based on handwriting.

another five years before the first book appeared in English. It was printed by William Caxton (1422–1491), who learned his trade in the German city of Cologne and printed his first books in Bruges. In 1476 he returned to London and set up a press at Westminster. He printed about 100 different books, including *The Canterbury Tales* by the English writer Geoffrey Chaucer.

In the 1490s another important printing workshop was set up in Venice by an Italian printer named Aldus Manutius (1449–1515). It was called the Aldine Press and specialized in producing beautiful editions of ancient Greek and Roman works by thinkers and writers like Sophocles, Homer, Aesop, Virgil, and Plato. The press also made pocket-sized books that were comparatively cheap and in 1502 published the Aldine edition of *The Divine Comedy* by the Italian poet Dante. Printing flourished everywhere, and by 1500 there were more than a thousand print shops in Europe.

ROMAN TYPE

The first letter cutters designed their characters to look like the beautiful handwriting that scribes had used. This design was called "black-letter type," or "Gothic." It was difficult to carve into metal molds and to read, and it took up a lot of space. However, some humanist scholars wrote in a simpler script that may have been used in ancient Rome and was certainly in use by the time of Charlemagne. German printers started making and using this "Roman type" in the 1460s, and it gradually took over from black-letter type. Around 1470 a French printer named Nicolas Jensen (1420–1480) designed and improved Roman type at his press in Venice. It became the new model for everyone.

SEE ALSO

♦ Biblical Studies
♦ Books and Libraries
♦ Literacy
♦ Literature

Prints

A print is an image made by pressing a sheet of paper onto an inked block or plate that has a design on it. During the Renaissance artists developed several printmaking techniques, and the prints they produced ranged from cheap pictures of popular religious subjects through book illustrations and reproductions of paintings to highly collectable prints that were works of art in their own right.

Printed images were popular and influential in the Renaissance because they were cheaper than other pictures such as paintings. Hundreds of identical prints could be made from a single plate. They were also easy to carry around and transport, which made them an effective way of spreading ideas as well as the fame of artists and their pictures.

Prints were made as early as the second century A.D. in China, though in Europe the first prints were made around 1400. In the Renaissance two main types of print were produced: woodcuts and line engravings.

WOODCUTS

Woodcut prints are made from wooden blocks. Various kinds of medium-soft wood, including cherry, pear, and beech, can be used to make the block. The artist draws the design onto the wood. The areas to be printed are left untouched, but the rest of the block is carved away using a gouge, knife, or chisel. When the design is finished, the block is covered in ink, then pressed

firmly against a piece of paper. The finished print is a reverse image of the design on the block.

In the Middle East woodcuts were used to print designs on cloth from the fifth century A.D. In Europe woodcut prints on paper date back to the late 14th century or early 15th century. The earliest surviving woodcut, a picture of Saint Christopher by an unknown artist, is dated 1423. During the 15th century woodcuts were mainly used to portray religious subjects such as Christ, Mary, and the saints. Prints were sold as souvenirs at fairs and pilgrimage centers. Woodcuts were also used to make books, called "block-books," in the first half of the 15th

Above: Albrecht Dürer's woodcut **The Fall of the Rebellious Angels** *(1498). It comes from a series of 16 prints he made to illustrate The* **Apocalypse,** *a collection of writings about Christ's second coming and the punishment of the wicked. The print is colored with watercolor paint.*

century. However, blockbooks were soon replaced by books printed using movable metal type, a quicker and easier method.

During the 16th century woodcuts were a popular means of producing pictures. Many early woodcuts were rather crude, but in the 16th century several artists—notably the German Albrecht Dürer—produced delicate woodcuts that were great works of art.

LINE ENGRAVINGS

In the Renaissance the other main technique used for printmaking was line engraving. In this method artists scratch their design onto the surface of a copper plate using a sharp tool called a burin. Ink is spread over the finished plate and worked into the scratched grooves, then the surface is wiped clean with a cloth. When the plate is pressed onto a piece of paper, the ink in the grooves produces an image on the paper, while the cleaned, smooth surface does not print. This printing method is called "intaglio."

More delicate effects can be produced in line engravings than woodcuts. Subtle tones (shades) can be achieved by scratching fine lines, dots, and areas of crosshatching (crossing

ENGRAVING IN ITALY

In Italy artists began to make line engravings around 1470, and the technique flourished in the 16th century. One of the first great Italian engravers was the Florentine painter, sculptor, and goldsmith Antonio Pollaiuolo (about 1432–1498). He ran a flourishing workshop with his brother Piero that produced paintings, bronzes, and prints. Pollaiuolo was interested in portraying the nude (unclothed) human form, and his engraving *Battle of the Nudes* (about

1489) is his best-known print. Like Leonardo da Vinci, Pollaiuolo is thought to have gained his knowledge of human anatomy by dissecting corpses.

Other great Italian printmakers include the painter Andrea Mantegna and Marcantonio Raimondi (about 1480–1534). Raimondi pioneered the use of prints to reproduce artists' work, a development that was of key importance in spreading the fame of Renaissance paintings and sculptures.

Left: Antonio Pollaiuolo, **Battle of the Nudes** *(about 1489). Pollaiuolo used the print to show his skill at depicting the human form— in the middle he shows front and back views of the same pose.*

lines) onto the copper plate. Line engraving developed after the woodcut, during the mid-15th century in Germany and the Netherlands, and later in Italy. The technique probably originated in goldsmiths' workshops, where craftsmen rubbed ink into the designs they had engraved on precious metals to check their work. One of the first engravers to produce prints that were works of art in their own right was the German artist Martin Schongauer (about 1445–1491).

ALBRECHT DÜRER

The German artist Albrecht Dürer (1471–1528) is widely acknowledged as the greatest printmaker of the Renaissance. He made more than 200 woodcuts and 100 line engravings, and excelled at both techniques.

When he was 15, Dürer was apprenticed to the German printmaker Michael Wolgemut, whose workshop made woodcut illustrations. A few years later, in 1490, Dürer traveled to the city of Colmar, hoping to work under Martin Schongauer, but arrived to find he had died. He then worked in Switzerland and Germany before traveling to Italy, where he saw prints by Andrea Mantegna and Antonio Pollaiuolo. Dürer was greatly inspired by Italian art and ideas, and he in turn was admired by leading Italian artists—the painter Raphael included several prints by Dürer among his most treasured possessions.

In 1498 Dürer produced *The Apocalypse*, the first of his great series of woodcuts, and between 1513 and 1514 made some of his finest engravings, including *Knight, Death, and the Devil*, *Melancolia*, and *Saint Jerome in His Study*. In these works he achieved a wealth of detail and a range of tone that few artists have matched.

The Dutch artist Lucas van Leyden (1494–1533) was one of many artists who was influenced by Dürer. A gifted youngster, van Leyden was already making fine engravings by the age of 14. During his relatively short life he produced a large number of engravings and woodcuts, including religious scenes full of the detail of everyday life.

ETCHING

Like Dürer, Lucas van Leyden also experimented with another intaglio printing technique: etching. In etching artists scratch their design onto a wax-covered metal plate to expose the metal. The plate is then dipped into acid, which eats into the exposed areas to produce the design in the metal.

Above: Dürer's engraving Saint Jerome in his Study *(1514). The print shows Dürer's skill at rendering detail and tone, for example, in the shadows cast by the tiny windowpanes.*

SEE ALSO
♦ Books and Libraries
♦ Dürer
♦ Mantegna
♦ Printing

Protestantism

The term "Protestantism" is used to describe the common beliefs and practices of a group of Christian churches. The earliest of them were established during the 16th century as part of a revolt against the Roman Catholic church. Protestantism developed into a separate branch of Christianity with a distinctive outlook, emphasizing the supreme authority of the Bible and the importance of personal faith.

Until the 16th century the Roman Catholic church was the single supreme religious body in western and central Europe. However, in 1517 it was openly challenged by the German monk Martin Luther (1483–1546). Luther criticized the widespread corruption within the church and also disagreed with many of its central beliefs. In particular he was opposed to the practice of selling indulgences, papal documents that were said to release the holders from punishment for their sins.

In the years following Luther's initial challenge to the church his views spread quickly across northern Europe. Lutherans did not see themselves as revolutionaries but as reformers, putting right what had gone wrong with the church. That is why the religious upheaval of the 16th century is called the Reformation.

THE DIET OF SPEYER

The term "Protestantism" only came to be used after the Diet of Speyer in 1529. The diet was a political assembly of the Holy Roman Empire and was made up of clerics, noblemen, and influential commoners. An earlier assembly had granted concessions to Luther's followers for political reasons. However, at the 1529 diet the Catholic majority declared that the rebels should no longer be tolerated. In reply the Lutheran minority issued a *Protestatio* ("protest"), from which they gained the name Protestants.

Later on the word Protestant was used to describe not only the Lutherans but also a number of other churches

Above: The inside of a Protestant church in the south of England. Its white walls, clear glass windows, and lack of ornament show the plain style that Protestants favored. In the 16th century many churches were stripped of their decoration and whitewashed inside.

Constantine, in which the first Christian emperor of Rome was said to have given spiritual and political authority to Pope Sylvester I. In the Renaissance scholars proved this document to be a forgery, a discovery that allowed Protestants to reject the pope's authority. The pope's position was also weakened by the Great Schism (1378–1417), a period when there were two popes, each claiming to be the rightful head of the church.

BASIC BELIEFS

Three other ideas were also central to all forms of Protestantism. One was that the Bible was the only authority on religious matters. This contradicted the Catholic view that the traditions and accumulated wisdom of the church were also important.

A second crucial idea was the doctrine of justification by faith alone, which stated that believers could not be saved by performing good deeds or through penances (acts of repentance) imposed by the church. People could only achieve salvation through the grace of God, which was a gift earned by Christ's sacrifice.

Another idea common to all Protestants was Luther's concept of the priesthood of all believers. Luther argued that all Christians had equal status and the same duties. Unlike Catholics, Protestants believed that the priest's office had no special, sacred character, and that the laity (nonclergy) should be full participants in church services, rather than just spectators.

In Protestant churches services became plainer, with more emphasis on readings and preaching. Services were no longer conducted in Latin but in the vernacular, or the everyday language of the congregation. The Bible itself began to be translated into

that had sprung up in opposition to Catholicism. Among them were the Calvinists and the Anabaptists. The exact beliefs of these different churches varied greatly, which often caused bitter arguments. However, they had enough in common to be seen as a single movement.

All Protestant churches rejected the authority of the pope in Rome. For centuries popes had argued that their authority as the supreme head of Christendom was derived from a document called the Donation of

THE BIBLE IN ENGLISH

The development of printing in the mid-15th century made the spread of translated versions of the Bible much easier. The first English version to be printed was the work of William Tyndale (about 1494–1536). An English humanist, Tyndale was forced to leave his country in 1524 because the church authorities refused to allow him to work on a translation in his native land. Based in Germany and the Low Countries, he began work on an English version of the New Testament and the Pentateuch, the first five books of the Old Testament. By 1526 his translation of the New Testament had been smuggled into England. However, he was captured and executed before he could finish his work on the Old Testament. His translation was completed by Miles Coverdale (about 1488–1569), another exile, who had assisted Tyndale in translating the Pentateuch. The Tyndale-Coverdale Bible became the first complete English Bible. It was published in 1535. A number of revised versions appeared later. Among them was the Great Bible of 1539, the first to be officially permitted in England. Tyndale and Coverdale's work provided the basis for the King James Bible, or the Authorized Version, which was prepared by a large committee of scholars and published in 1611. This version was read by English-speaking Protestants for hundreds of years.

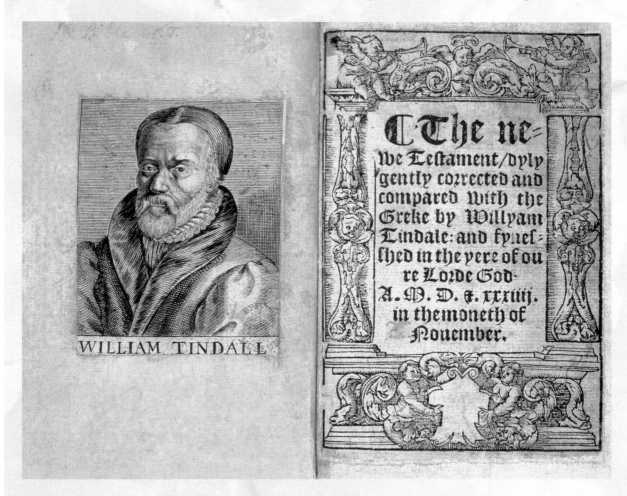

Above: The title page from William Tyndale's translation of the New Testament. Tyndale translated the New Testament from Greek into English in 1525; the book shown here is a revised version printed in 1534.

many different languages, so that people could read and interpret it themselves. Translations and adaptations of Latin texts such as Luther's Bible, Thomas Cranmer's *Book of Common Prayer*, and the King James version of the Bible were among the literary masterpieces of the Renaissance.

THE CEREMONY OF MASS

Many other complex issues separated Catholics from Protestants. Some of them also caused splits between Protestants. For example, Catholics believed that during the ceremony of Mass (the Eucharist) the bread and wine used in the ritual literally turned into the body and blood of Christ. Protestant churches modified this doctrine in different ways, although only the Swiss religious reformer Huldrych Zwingli (1484–1531) and his followers denied that any change took place at all. They argued that the Eucharist was a simple ceremony of commemoration. The disputes that followed were bitter and had significant consequences which prevented Luther and Zwingli from forging an alliance against their common enemies.

THE QUESTION OF FREE WILL

Another vital doctrinal issue was the question of whether or not human beings had enough free will (choice) to determine their salvation or damnation, that is, whether their souls went to heaven or hell after death. Catholic thinkers had not always taken the same view about this question, but the generally accepted opinion was that, although God was all-powerful, humans had been left free to make a choice between good and evil.

Luther's beliefs about free will became widely known when he conducted a fierce debate on the

subject with the great Dutch humanist writer Desiderius Erasmus (about 1466–1536), who believed in the role of human choice in salvation. Luther argued that the ultimate fate of every human being was decided before he or she was born and that people could not achieve salvation through their own actions. This belief is called the doctrine of predestination. At first almost all Protestant churches accepted the idea of predestination, but from the early 17th century a number of them modified their position.

Because of their stress on Bible reading Protestants tended to develop divergent opinions. In the years following the Reformation hundreds of separate Protestant churches and sects developed. This fragmentation continued for centuries.

Above: The Swiss reformer Huldrych Zwingli. Zwingli's church was stricter than Luther's and abolished the Mass.

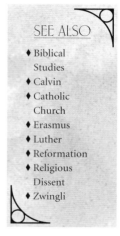

SEE ALSO

♦ Biblical
  Studies
♦ Calvin
♦ Catholic
  Church
♦ Erasmus
♦ Luther
♦ Reformation
♦ Religious
  Dissent
♦ Zwingli

Raphael

Above: Most scholars agree that this painting is an early self-portrait by Raphael. It was probably made around 1506, when Raphael was in Florence, and shows him as a young man looking thoughtfully out of the picture.

At the beginning of the 16th century Raphael (1483–1520) was one of three artists who brought a new grandeur to the period that is now called the High Renaissance (about 1500–1530). The others were Leonardo da Vinci (1452–1519) and Michelangelo (1475–1564). Raphael worked mainly as a painter, and his pictures combine harmony and balance with human warmth and tenderness. He was known in his own lifetime as the "Prince of Painters," and his style remained a model for painters for centuries to come.

Raphael Sanzio was born in 1483 in Urbino, a hilltop city in central Italy ruled by the Montefeltro family. The Montefeltro encouraged Renaissance culture and attracted leading painters to their court, including Piero della Francesca. Raphael's father, Giovanni Santi, was himself a painter and writer, and gave his son his first lessons in painting as well as a grounding in the thought of the Renaissance scholars known as the humanists.

Both of Raphael's parents died before he reached the age of 12. Raphael had already shown himself to be a gifted artist, however, and soon after his father's death he went to Perugia, a city in the neighboring region of Umbria. He was probably attracted to the city by the reputation of its most celebrated painter, Perugino, a former pupil of Piero della Francesca. It is likely that by 1500 Raphael was working as one of Perugino's assistants.

Perugino's clear, simple style contrasted with the elaborateness of much of the art of the time and had a lasting effect on Raphael's work. By 1504, however, the 21-year-old Raphael was already surpassing the older artist. Such works as *The Marriage of the Virgin* (about 1504) show how Raphael portrayed the people in his pictures with tender expressions and graceful poses, even when he borrowed Perugino's rather stiff compositions or arrangements. All through his career Raphael was able to absorb into his own art the qualities that he admired in the work of other painters.

THE FLORENTINE PERIOD

In 1504 Raphael left Perugia for Florence. At this time Florence still stood at the forefront of developments

THE VIRGIN AND CHILD

Raphael painted the Virgin and Child throughout his life, and his paintings of the theme remain among his best-loved works. In his early pictures Raphael showed the Virgin as a young, loving mother gazing tenderly at her son. Most earlier painters had depicted the Virgin as queenly and remote, sometimes showing her seated on a throne or floating above her worshipers. Raphael, by contrast, made the Virgin seem more familiar and human, depicting her, the child Jesus, and sometimes the young John the Baptist sitting together in lush, sunlit landscapes.

Raphael arranged the figures in a pyramid shape, with the Virgin placing her arm tenderly around Jesus. He also used a few dominant colors, such as blue and red, to give a sense of balance and calm in the picture. Such harmonies suggest a higher, sacred world, removed from the chaos and disorder of everyday life.

After Raphael moved to Rome, his treatment of the theme became grander and more austere. This change was partly because his paintings were now intended for imposing settings—such as large churches and the papal palace of the Vatican—and partly because he was influenced by the powerful art of Michelangelo. For example, *The Sistine Madonna,* painted in about 1513 to hang over the bier (coffin stand) of Pope Julius II, shows the Virgin as the Queen of Heaven stepping down through the clouds. Yet despite the splendor of the painting, it is still full of human feeling. The Virgin appears kind and gentle, while two chubby putti (baby angels) sadly contemplate Julius's death.

Above: **The Madonna of the Goldfinch** *(about 1505)* **by Raphael. The Christ child holds a goldfinch, a** *traditional symbol of his future suffering.*

in Italian art and particularly of the grand new styles being developed by Leonardo and Michelangelo. Raphael probably saw the portrait by Leonardo that we today know as the *Mona Lisa* (1503–1506) and Michelangelo's heroic sculpture of David (1501–1504), which stood in one of Florence's main public squares. He was also inspired by the work of another Florentine artist, Fra Bartolommeo, who painted solemn, richly colored altarpieces.

In Florence Raphael concentrated on painting intimate, small-scale pictures of the Virgin and Child (Mary and Jesus). Wealthy individuals often commissioned artists to make such paintings to display in their homes, where they were an aid to prayer and meditation. Raphael's paintings of the theme were quite different from anything produced before, however. He took his initial inspiration from Leonardo, borrowing his soft, hazy forms, gently smiling figures, and powerful, pyramidlike compositions. However, he gave his paintings a fresh, intimate quality that was altogether different from the mysterious, other-worldly feel found in Leonardo's paintings. While Leonardo shrouded his figures in misty twilight, Raphael often bathed his in summery sunshine. And while Leonardo set his figures against a dramatic landscape of craggy mountains, Raphael preferred settings of well-tended fields, sparkling rivers, and homely villages.

RAPHAEL IN ROME

In 1508 Pope Julius II (pope 1503–1513) summoned Raphael to Rome. Julius was determined to turn Rome into a splendid city once again, after years of neglect. His chief architect and artistic adviser was Donato Bramante (1444–1514), who in 1506 began the rebuilding of Saint Peter's, Rome's main church. Bramante had trained in Urbino, and it was probably he who recommended Raphael to Julius.

Raphael's first task in Rome was to decorate a series of rooms in the pope's private apartments in the Vatican. The decorated rooms became so famous that they were known simply as the *Stanze* (Italian for "rooms"). For each room the pope chose a subject or theme, which Raphael illustrated in a series of grandiose frescoes. The most

Left: A cartoon (design) by Raphael for a tapestry showing the miraculous draft of fish, a Bible story in which Christ tells the apostle Peter and his friends to lower their fishing nets, which are then miraculously filled with fish. It is one of a series of tapestries that Pope Leo X asked Raphael to design for the Sistine Chapel. Raphael completed the cartoons in 1516, and the tapestries were woven in Brussels.

THE SCHOOL OF ATHENS

The fresco (a wall painting made on wet, or "fresh," plaster) illustrating ancient learning in the Stanza della Segnatura is one of Raphael's greatest works and one of the finest achievements of Renaissance art. It covers the whole of one arched wall and shows a gathering of ancient Greek thinkers and scientists. In reality the great men shown lived at many different times, but Raphael brings them all together in a magnificent imaginary building of soaring arches and larger-than-life statues. Because Athens was considered the center of ancient Greek learning, the painting is usually known as *The School of Athens* (1510–1511). There are more than 50 figures, all shown in different poses. At the center, framed by a distant arch, are Plato (on the left) and Aristotle (on the right), the greatest ancient thinkers. Plato points heavenward, indicating his concern with the higher world of ideas, while Aristotle gestures downward, suggesting his interest in the "earthly" or practical sciences. The brooding man sitting on the bottom step represents the Greek philosopher Heraclitus but is said to be a portrait of Michelangelo. Despite the great number and variety of figures, Raphael managed to create a unified, serene composition. For all the lively detail, the viewer's eyes are drawn up the steps to the focus of the painting: the philosophers Plato and Aristotle.

Above: The School of Athens, *painted by Raphael between 1510 and 1511. Among the great thinkers shown are Euclid, who bends down with a pair of compasses on the right; Ptolemy, who stands to the right of Euclid holding a starry sphere; and Pythagoras, who sits writing on the left with a blackboard at his feet.*

celebrated room, the Stanza della Segnatura (originally Julius's study but named after a law court that later met there), deals with the relationship between ancient Greek philosophy and the Christian religion. The frescoes for all the rooms took some nine years to complete, although Raphael painted only the first two himself. By the time work began on the third room in 1514, he was so busy on other projects that he had to leave the actual painting to a team of trusted assistants.

THE POPE'S FAVORITE ARTIST

Raphael quickly became the pope's favorite artist. Unlike the moody, irritable Michelangelo, who at this time was working on the ceiling of the Sistine Chapel, Raphael was charming, kind, and friendly. His friends included some of the most brilliant thinkers, poets, and statesmen of the age; and he painted insightful portraits of some of them, including the humanist and poet Baldassare Castiglione (1478–1529). Raphael's popularity continued under Julius's successor, Leo X (pope 1513–1521), who after Bramante's death in 1514 appointed him his chief artistic adviser and architect for Saint Peter's.

Although the pope kept Raphael very busy, the artist also found time to carry out work for other people. In about 1511, for example, he painted some pretty frescoes with subjects drawn from ancient Greek and Roman myths in a villa belonging to a banker called Agostino Chigi, for whom he also designed a richly decorated chapel (begun in about 1512). To complete all his commissions, Raphael needed the help of a workshop of apprentices and assistants. Nevertheless, scholars think that much of the work that survives from this time was painted by Raphael himself rather than by his workshop.

In 1520, on his 37th birthday, Raphael died, plunging the pope and his whole court into mourning. At the time of his death Raphael was working on a large altarpiece depicting the Transfiguration (the moment when Christ reveals his divine nature to his disciples). The unfinished painting was displayed above Raphael's bier during his funeral and was later completed by his most gifted assistant, Giulio Romano. The altarpiece is full of drama and violence, and scholars think that it indicates that Raphael was evolving a new style, one that later artists developed into mannerism.

Above: Raphael's last painting, **The Transfiguration** *(1517–1520).*

SEE ALSO

- Leonardo da Vinci
- Michelangelo
- Mannerism
- Mythological Art
- Painting
- Saint Peter's, Rome

Reformation

Above: A 19th-century painting of Martin Luther nailing his 95 theses to the church door in Wittenberg. The act sparked off the Reformation.

At the beginning of the 16th century the Catholic church was rich and powerful. The pope, who was head of the church, owned lands and lived in luxury as if he were an Italian prince rather than a man of the church. Other churchmen were also wealthy, sometimes holding several church posts at the same time, which meant they could not fulfill all their duties properly. These and other abuses led humanist scholars to call for reform, but it took the outrage of a German monk, Martin Luther, to start a widespread protest movement. Luther's beliefs led him to form a separate "Protestant" church that flourished particularly in northern Europe. This break from Catholicism is called the Reformation.

The Catholic church believed that everyone was a sinner (someone who offends against religious or moral law). However, anyone could be forgiven and could go to heaven if they carried out penances (acts of devotion or self-denial). Only a priest could order the penances that freed a person from their sins. By 1500 the Catholic church was frequently accused of abusing this power. Priests encouraged people to believe that they could buy their way to heaven by purchasing a slip of paper called an indulgence, which was supposed to cancel a person's sins.

TETZEL AND LUTHER

In 1517 Pope Leo X authorized the sale of indulgences to raise money to rebuild the church of Saint Peter's in Rome. A Dominican monk called Johann Tetzel was appointed by the archbishop of Mainz to travel through Germany selling indulgences. His aggressive and persuasive salesmanship outraged Martin Luther, who drew up 95 theses (statements) outlining everything that was corrupt about the Catholic church. He nailed them to the

THE EUCHARIST

The issue that caused most disagreement among the new Protestant churches was the question of what actually happened during the Eucharist—the communion service (Mass) that commemorates Christ's Last Supper with his disciples. According to the Bible, Christ gave his disciples bread and wine, saying, "This is my body and blood." Catholics believed that the bread and wine held up by the priest during the Mass were mystically transformed into the body and blood of Christ. Luther did not believe in this mystical transformation, but he did believe that Christ was present in the bread and wine. Other Protestants did not believe there was anything special about the bread and wine.

door of the castle church in Wittenberg on October 31. This was an accepted way to invite debate.

Luther was a professor of theology (religious thought) at Wittenberg University. He was angered by the corruption and abuses of the church, and he had also thought deeply about the church's teachings. He had concluded that a person could only understand God's wishes properly by studying the text of the Bible for him or herself. The church, however, held that only churchmen could interpret the Bible. At that time the Bible was generally only available in Greek or Latin, which ordinary people could not understand.

This doctrine—that the Bible is the sole authority and can be read and interpreted by anyone—was known as *sola scriptura*. It brought Luther into a head-on collision with the church, as did his second doctrine, known as *sola fide*. *Sola fide* concerned the way people can be saved, that is, go to heaven after they die. The church taught that living a good life and performing good works would help a person toward salvation. Luther, however, came to believe that people could only be saved by their faith. His view was based on the Bible's teaching that Christ died on the cross to save people from their sins. Luther thought it was only necessary to believe in this in order to be saved.

Right: A woodcut by Lucas Cranach the Elder (1472–1553) showing the pope acting as a moneychanger while selling indulgences. The sale of indulgences so angered Martin Luther that he drew up a list of corruptions in the church that started the Reformation.

INVITING DEBATE

By pinning his theses to the church door, Luther was doing what many others had done before him to invite debate. He had no intention of breaking with the church at this stage. However, in 1518 Luther was summoned to Rome to face a charge of heresy, or wrong belief. His university stepped in to protect him, and instead, Luther and Johann Eck (the pope's representative) held a memorable debate at Leipzig in 1519. In it Luther asserted that the pope and church councils could be wrong, and that scripture was the sole authority. These assertions alone condemned him as a heretic. In June 1520 he was excommunicated (expelled) from the Catholic church.

REFORMERS AND HUMANISTS

There had been earlier attempts to reform the church. In the late 15th century several new orders of begging friars arose in Spain and Italy, dedicated to a life of poverty. Individual reformers had also paved the way for Luther. John Wycliffe, a 14th-century English reformer, had challenged the authority of the pope and attracted much support. One of his followers, a Bohemian (Czech) called Jan Hus, was burned at the stake for his beliefs in 1415. His supporters fought on against the authorities in the Hussite Wars.

The Dutch humanist Desiderius Erasmus (1466–1536) had attacked abuses and superstitions in the Catholic church long before Luther's 95 theses. Like other humanists, he had been inspired by earlier thinkers. He translated and published editions of classical authors and early church fathers as well as writing his own works advocating reform.

In this way the Reformation grew out of the new spirit of inquiry that characterized the Renaissance. One innovation that helped the spread of reforming ideas was the printing press. Luther used it to great effect, pouring out books, pamphlets, and sermons for 30 years. His pamphlets, which were written in German, reached a wide audience, and his energetic, populist writing style won him many followers.

THE DIET OF WORMS

By the time Charles V became Holy Roman emperor in 1519, several German princes within the empire were sympathetic to Luther's ideas,

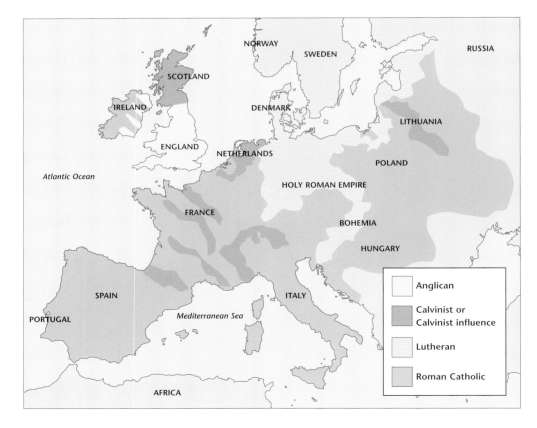

Left: A map of Europe showing the spread of Protestant churches in the mid-16th century. Lutheranism was strong in the Holy Roman Empire and Scandinavia, while Calvinism had taken hold of the Netherlands, parts of France, and Scotland. England and parts of Ireland were Anglican, although much of the population remained true to the Catholic faith.

partly because they promised to weaken the power of the emperor. Luther had returned to Wittenberg in Saxony, where the elector (ruler) Frederick the Wise supported and protected him. Luther continued to publish revolutionary pamphlets in which he challenged the authority of the pope and condemned abuses in the church. Eventually Charles V was driven to take action. In January 1521 he summoned Luther to defend his ideas at the Diet (assembly) of Worms before the electors of Germany and the pope's representative.

Luther was under a sentence of death as a heretic and would be in danger once he left Saxony. So Charles agreed to give him safe conduct to Worms. In every town Luther passed through, people cheered him—the popularity of Luther's message was very clear. At Worms Luther was unrepentant. After stating his case, he ended his speech, "Here I stand; I can do no other: God help me, Amen." The diet denounced Luther's ideas as heresy; his life was now in extreme danger. On the way back to Wittenberg he was ambushed by friends and taken to a safe castle, where he remained for the next eight months.

Since he was now an outcast from the Catholic church, Luther was forced to establish his own church.

THE LUTHERAN CHURCH

Luther's breakaway church retained a traditional structure of bishops and clergy, but conducted services in the local language rather than Latin. Luther's mixture of radical ideas and conservative practice proved very popular in Germany; and despite the edict of Worms, many German rulers and cities embraced Lutheranism.

In 1526 the diet met at Speyer and, in the absence of the emperor, issued a

Above: A 19th-century artist's impression of Luther addressing the Diet of Worms in 1521. The diet was unconvinced by Luther's statement and denounced him as a heretic in what is known as the Edict of Worms.

THE ANABAPTISTS

One group of reformers insisted that the text of the Bible should be followed strictly to the letter. They believed that people should only be baptized as adults, since that is how it had been in Jesus' time. For this reason they were nicknamed "Anabaptists."

Anabaptists rejected the established social order, with its idea of property, and refused to pay taxes. They were persecuted for their revolutionary ideas in Protestant and Catholic countries alike. In 1533 a group of Anabaptists took over the city of Munster in northern Germany and began a purge of sinners in preparation for Christ's second coming on earth. They practiced polygamy (having more than one wife), seized property, and killed anyone who would not be baptized. The bloodbath ended in 1535, when the citizens of Munster turned on the Anabaptists and killed them.

From that time Anabaptists were even more harshly persecuted throughout Europe. Many of them emigrated to North America in the 17th century.

decree stating that each ruler or city could decide for themselves whether to follow Catholicism or Lutheranism. However, at a second Diet of Speyer held in 1529 this decree was repealed, and Lutheranism once again outlawed. After the diet six Lutheran princes and 14 imperial cities signed a "protest" against the ruling. This is the origin of the world "Protestant."

Lutheranism was formally defined by a supporter of Luther's, Philip Melanchthon, in a document called the *Augsburg Confession*, which was presented to the emperor at the Diet of Augsburg in 1530. It was intended to offer a compromise to the emperor, but it failed. Lutheranism remained officially outlawed. Nevertheless, Lutheranism continued to spread in Germany, and the conflict between Catholicism and Lutheranism caused many wars of religion over the ensuing years.

ZWINGLI AND CALVIN

In other parts of Europe reformers appeared who challenged aspects of Lutheran doctrine and practice and set up their own churches. One of these reformers was Huldrych Zwingli (1484–1531), who set up a reformed church in Zurich, Switzerland, between 1523 and 1525. Zwingli's church was more radical than Luther's. All images (paintings and statues) were swept away, and the ceremony of Mass was abolished. Zwingli's reformation spread swiftly through Switzerland, and in 1529 Luther and Zwingli met at Marburg to debate their views on the

THE ENGLISH REFORMATION

In England the break from the Catholic church was sparked by a constitutional crisis. King Henry VIII (ruled 1509–1547) was married to Catherine of Aragon, but by 1529 she was beyond childbearing age and had failed to provide him with a son. Henry wanted to marry the much younger Anne Boleyn and produce an heir. He argued that his marriage to Catherine was invalid because she was his brother Arthur's widow.

Henry asked Pope Clement VII to grant him a divorce; when it was refused, he ordered a team of scholars to scour the Bible for evidence to support his case. One of Henry's ministers, Thomas Cromwell, encouraged the king to believe he could set up a separate, independent church in England, which he would head instead of the pope. That would mean he could grant himself a divorce. In January 1533 Henry married Anne Boleyn secretly, and later the same year Thomas Cranmer, archbishop of Canterbury, declared that Henry's marriage to Catherine was invalid. The following year an act of Parliament established the Church of England, with the king as its supreme head.

Henry was not against Catholicism—just against the pope. His Church of England was neither specifically Protestant nor Catholic, and that was to be a problem for English politics for the next 150 years.

Left: Henry VIII of England, whose desire for an heir led to a break with the pope and the Roman Catholic church.

Left: A fresco (wall painting) of Huldrych Zwingli preaching in Zurich. Zwingli was an even more radical reformer than Luther, and from 1523 his church quickly became established in Switzerland.

Eucharist or Mass (see box on page 63). Luther believed Christ was physically present in the Eucharist since Christ is present everywhere. Zwingli argued that the Mass was simply a ceremony commemorating the Last Supper. The attempt to form an alliance between Swiss Protestants and Lutherans failed on this point of doctrine.

After Zwingli's death in 1531 Zurich declined in importance, and John Calvin became leader of the Swiss Reformation in Geneva. Calvin was a Frenchman who was banned from France for his radical beliefs in 1534. In 1536 he published his *Institutes of the Christian Religion*, which described his form of Protestantism, including his doctrine of predestination, which said that God had predestined some people to be saved (the elect) and others to be damned. According to Calvin, nothing that anyone did during their lifetime could change this.

Calvin arrived in Geneva in 1542 and was invited by the city authorities to stay and set up a reformed church there. Calvin set up a form of church government in the city. Calvinist Geneva was austere and godly—swearing, gambling, dancing, and extravagant dress were punishable crimes. Calvinist churches were very plain, without any ornament. Calvin also did away with the hierarchy of the church. Instead of popes, bishops, and the clergy, the church was run by ministers chosen by their congregations and a group of elders who were elected laymen (nonclergy).

The Calvinist religion spread to other parts of Europe and beyond. One reformer who was strongly influenced by Calvin was John Knox, who led the Reformation in Scotland, creating the Presbyterian religion. Calvinism also became popular in the Netherlands and in pockets of France.

SEE ALSO

♦ Biblical Studies
♦ Calvin
♦ Catholic Church
♦ Counter Reformation
♦ Erasmus
♦ Henry VIII
♦ Luther
♦ Protestantism
♦ Religious Dissent
♦ Zwingli

Timeline

♦ **1305** Giotto begins work on frescoes for the Arena Chapel, Padua—he is often considered the father of Renaissance art.

♦ **1321** Dante publishes the *Divine Comedy*, which has a great influence on later writers.

♦ **1327** Petrarch begins writing the sonnets known as the *Canzoniere*.

♦ **1337** The start of the Hundred Years' War between England and France.

♦ **1353** Boccaccio writes the *Decameron*, an influential collection of 100 short stories.

♦ **1368** The Ming dynasty comes to power in China.

♦ **1377** Pope Gregory XI moves the papacy back to Rome from Avignon, where it has been based since 1309.

♦ **1378** The Great Schism begins: two popes, Urban VI and Clement VII, both lay claim to the papacy.

♦ **1378** English theologian John Wycliffe criticizes the practices of the Roman Catholic church.

♦ **1380** Ivan I of Muscovy defeats the army of the Mongol Golden Horde at the battle of Kulikovo.

♦ **1389** The Ottomans defeat the Serbs at the battle of Kosovo, beginning a new phase of Ottoman expansion.

♦ **1397** Sigismund of Hungary is defeated by the Ottoman Turks at the battle of Nicopolis.

♦ **1397** Queen Margaret of Denmark unites Denmark, Sweden, and Norway under the Union of Kalmar.

♦ **1398** The Mongol leader Tamerlane invades India.

♦ **1399** Henry Bolingbroke becomes Henry IV of England.

♦ **1400** English writer Geoffrey Chaucer dies, leaving his *Canterbury Tales* unfinished.

♦ **1403** In Italy the sculptor Ghiberti wins a competition to design a new set of bronze doors for Florence Cathedral.

♦ **c.1402** The Bohemian preacher Jan Hus begins to attack the corruption of the church.

♦ **1405** The Chinese admiral Cheng Ho commands the first of seven expeditions to the Indian Ocean and East Africa.

♦ **1415** Jan Hus is summoned to the Council of Constance and condemned to death.

♦ **1415** Henry V leads the English to victory against the French at the battle of Agincourt.

♦ **c.1415** Florentine sculptor Donatello produces his sculpture *Saint George*.

♦ **1416** Venice defeats the Ottoman fleet at the battle of Gallipoli, but does not check the Ottoman advance.

♦ **1417** The Council of Constance elects Martin V pope, ending the Great Schism.

♦ **1418** Brunelleschi designs the dome of Florence Cathedral.

♦ **1420** Pope Martin V returns the papacy to Rome, bringing peace and order to the city.

♦ **c.1420** Prince Henry of Portugal founds a school of navigation at Sagres, beginning a great age of Portuguese exploration.

♦ **1422** Charles VI of France dies, leaving his throne to the English king Henry VI. Charles VI's son also claims the throne.

♦ **c.1425** Florentine artist Masaccio paints the *Holy Trinity*, the first painting to use the new science of perspective.

♦ **1429** Joan of Arc leads the French to victory at Orléans; Charles VII is crowned king of France in Reims Cathedral.

♦ **1431** The English burn Joan of Arc at the stake for heresy.

♦ **1433** Sigismund of Luxembourg becomes Holy Roman emperor.

♦ **1434** Cosimo de Medici comes to power in Florence.

♦ **1434** The Flemish artist Jan van Eyck paints the *Arnolfini Marriage* using the newly developed medium of oil paint.

♦ **1439** The Council of Florence proclaims the reunion of the Western and Orthodox churches.

♦ **c.1440** Donatello completes his statue of David—the first life-size bronze sculpture since antiquity.

♦ **1443** Federigo da Montefeltro becomes ruler of Urbino.

♦ **1447** The Milanese people declare their city a republic.

♦ **1450** The condottiere Francesco Sforza seizes control of Milan.

♦ **1450** Fra Angelico paints *The Annunciation* for the monastery of San Marco in Florence.

♦ **1453** Constantinople, capital of the Byzantine Empire, falls to the Ottomans and becomes the capital of the Muslim Empire.

♦ **1453** The French defeat the English at the battle of Castillon, ending the Hundred Years' War.

♦ **1454–1456** Venice, Milan, Florence, Naples, and the papacy form the Italian League to maintain peace in Italy.

♦ **1455** The start of the Wars of the Roses between the Houses of York and Lancaster in England.

♦ **c.1455** The German Johannes Gutenberg develops the first printing press using movable type.

♦ **1456** The Florentine painter Uccello begins work on the *Battle of San Romano*.

♦ **1461** The House of York wins the Wars of the Roses; Edward IV becomes king of England.

♦ **1461** Sonni Ali becomes king of the Songhai Empire in Africa.

♦ **1462** Marsilio Ficino founds the Platonic Academy of Florence—the birthplace of Renaissance Neoplatonism.

♦ **1463** War breaks out between Venice and the Ottoman Empire.

♦ **1465** The Italian painter Mantegna begins work on the Camera degli Sposi in Mantua.

♦ **1467** Civil war breaks out in Japan, lasting for over a century.

♦ **1469** Lorenzo the Magnificent, grandson of Cosimo de Medici, comes to power in Florence.

♦ **1469** The marriage of Isabella I of Castile and Ferdinand V of Aragon unites the two kingdoms.

♦ **1470** The Florentine sculptor Verrocchio completes his *David*.

♦ **1476** William Caxton establishes the first English printing press at Westminster, near London.

♦ **1477** Pope Sixtus IV begins building the Sistine Chapel.

♦ **c.1477** Florentine painter Sandro Botticelli paints the *Primavera*, one of the first large-scale mythological paintings of the Renaissance.

♦ **1478** The Spanish Inquisition is founded in Spain.

♦ **1480** The Ottoman fleet destroys the port of Otranto in south Italy.

♦ **1485** Henry Tudor becomes Henry VII of England—the start of the Tudor dynasty.

♦ **1486** *The Witches' Hammer* is published, a handbook on how to hunt down witches.

♦ **1488** Portuguese navigator Bartholomeu Dias reaches the Cape of Good Hope.

♦ **1491** Missionaries convert King Nzina Nkowu of the Congo to Christianity.

♦ **1492** The Spanish monarchs conquer Granada, the last Moorish territory in Spain.

♦ **1492** Christopher Columbus lands in the Bahamas, claiming the territory for Spain.

♦ **1492** Henry VII of England renounces all English claims to the French throne.

♦ **1493** The Hapsburg Maximilian becomes Holy Roman emperor.

♦ **1494** Charles VIII of France invades Italy, beginning four decades of Italian wars.

♦ **1494** In Italy Savonarola comes to power in Florence.

♦ **1494** The Treaty of Tordesillas divides the non-Christian world between Spain and Portugal.

♦ **1495** Leonardo da Vinci begins work on *The Last Supper* .

♦ **1495** Spain forms a Holy League with the Holy Roman emperor and expels the French from Naples.

♦ **1498** Portuguese navigator Vasco da Gama reaches Calicut, India.

♦ **1498** German artist Dürer creates the *Apocalypse* woodcuts.

♦ **1500** Portuguese navigator Pedro Cabral discovers Brazil.

♦ **c.1500–1510** Dutch painter Hieronymous Bosch paints *The Garden of Earthly Delights*.

♦ **c.1502** Italian architect Donato Bramante designs the Tempietto Church in Rome.

♦ **1503** Leonardo da Vinci begins painting the *Mona Lisa*.

♦ **1504** Michelangelo finishes his statue of David, widely seen as a symbol of Florence.

♦ **c.1505** Venetian artist Giorgione paints *The Tempest*.

♦ **1506** The Italian architect Donato Bramante begins work on rebuilding Saint Peter's, Rome.

♦ **1508** Michelangelo begins work on the ceiling of the Sistine Chapel in the Vatican.

♦ **1509** Henry VIII ascends the throne of England.

♦ **1509** The League of Cambrai defeats Venice at the battle of Agnadello.

♦ **1510–1511** Raphael paints *The School of Athens* in the Vatican.

♦ **1511** The French are defeated at the battle of Ravenna in Italy and are forced to retreat over the Alps.

♦ **1513** Giovanni de Medici becomes Pope Leo X.

♦ **1515** Thomas Wolsey becomes lord chancellor of England.

♦ **1515** Francis I becomes king of France. He invades Italy and captures Milan.

♦ **c.1515** German artist Grünewald paints the *Isenheim Altarpiece*.

♦ **1516** Charles, grandson of the emperor Maximilian I, inherits the Spanish throne as Charles I.

♦ **1516** Thomas More publishes his political satire *Utopia*.

♦ **1516** Dutch humanist Erasmus publishes a more accurate version of the Greek New Testament.

♦ **1517** Martin Luther pins his 95 theses on the door of the castle church in Wittenburg.

♦ **1519** Charles I of Spain becomes Holy Roman emperor Charles V.

♦ **1519–1521** Hernán Cortés conquers Mexico for Spain.

♦ **1520** Henry VIII of England and Francis I of France meet at the Field of the Cloth of Gold to sign a treaty of friendship.

♦ **1520** Portuguese navigator Ferdinand Magellan discovers a route to the Indies around the tip of South America.

♦ **1520** Süleyman the Magnificent becomes ruler of the Ottoman Empire, which now dominates the eastern Mediterranean.

♦ **1520–1523** Titian paints *Bacchus and Ariadne* for Alfonso d'Este.

♦ **1521** Pope Leo X excommuicates Martin Luther.

♦ **1521** The emperor Charles V attacks France, beginning a long period of European war.

♦ **1522** Ferdinand Magellan's ship the *Victoria* is the first to sail around the world.

♦ **1523–1525** Huldrych Zwingli sets up a Protestant church at Zurich in Switzerland.

♦ **1525** In Germany the Peasants' Revolt is crushed, and its leader, Thomas Münzer, is executed.

♦ **1525** The emperor Charles V defeats the French at the battle of Pavia and takes Francis I prisoner.

♦ **1525** William Tyndale translates the New Testament into English.

♦ **1526** The Ottoman Süleyman the Magnificent defeats Hungary at the battle of Mohács.

♦ **1526** Muslim Mongol leader Babur invades northern India and establishes the Mogul Empire.

♦ **c.1526** The Italian artist Correggio paints the *Assumption of the Virgin* in Parma Cathedral.

♦ **1527** Charles V's armies overrun Italy and sack Rome.

♦ **1527–1530** Gustavus I founds a Lutheran state church in Sweden.

♦ **1528** Italian poet and humanist Baldassare Castiglione publishes *The Courtier*.

♦ **1529** The Ottoman Süleyman the Magnificent lays siege to Vienna, but eventually retreats.

♦ **1530** The Catholic church issues the "Confutation," attacking Luther and Protestantism.

♦ **1531** The Protestant princes of Germany form the Schmalkaldic League.

♦ **1531–1532** Francisco Pizarro conquers Peru for Spain.

♦ **1532** Machiavelli's *The Prince* is published after his death.

♦ **1533** Henry VIII of England rejects the authority of the pope and marries Anne Boleyn.

♦ **1533** Anabaptists take over the city of Münster in Germany.

♦ **1533** Christian III of Denmark founds the Lutheran church of Denmark.

♦ **1534** Paul III becomes pope and encourages the growth of new religious orders such as the Jesuits.

♦ **1534** Luther publishes his German translation of the Bible.

♦ **1534** The Act of Supremacy declares Henry VIII supreme head of the Church of England.

♦ **c.1535** Parmigianino paints the mannerist masterpiece *Madonna of the Long Neck*.

♦ **1535–1536** The Swiss city of Geneva becomes Protestant and expels the Catholic clergy.

♦ **1536** Calvin publishes *Institutes of the Christian Religion*, which sets out his idea of predestination.

♦ **1536** Pope Paul III sets up a reform commission to examine the state of the Catholic church.

♦ **1537** Hans Holbein is appointed court painter to Henry VIII of England.

♦ **1539** Italian painter Bronzino begins working for Cosimo de Medici the Younger in Florence.

♦ **1539** Ignatius de Loyola founds the Society of Jesus (the Jesuits).

♦ **1541** John Calvin sets up a model Christian city in Geneva.

♦ **1543** Andreas Vesalius publishes *On the Structure of the Human Body*, a handbook of anatomy based on dissections.

♦ **1543** Polish astronomer Copernicus's *On the Revolutions of the Heavenly Spheres* proposes a sun-centered universe.

♦ **1544** Charles V and Francis I of France sign the Truce of Crespy.

♦ **1545** Pope Paul III organizes the Council of Trent to counter the threat of Protestantism.

♦ **1545** Spanish explorers find huge deposits of silver in the Andes Mountains of Peru.

♦ **1547** Charles V defeats the Protestant Schmalkaldic League at the Battle of Mühlberg.

♦ **1547** Ivan IV "the Terrible" declares himself czar of Russia.

♦ **1548** Titian paints the equestrian portrait *Charles V after the Battle of Mühlberg*.

♦ **1548** Tintoretto paints *Saint Mark Rescuing the Slave*.

♦ **1550** Italian Georgio Vasari publishes his *Lives of the Artists*.

♦ **1553** Mary I of England restores the Catholic church.

♦ **1554** Work begins on the Cathedral of Saint Basil in Red Square, Moscow.

♦ **1555** At the Peace of Augsburg Charles V allows the German princes to determine their subjects' religion.

♦ **1556** Ivan IV defeats the last Mongol khanates. Muscovy now dominates the Volga region.

♦ **1556** Philip II becomes king of Spain.

♦ **1559** Elizabeth I of England restores the Protestant church.

♦ **1562** The Wars of Religion break out in France.

♦ **1565** Flemish artist Pieter Bruegel the Elder paints *Hunters in the Snow*.

♦ **1565** Italian architect Palladio designs the Villa Rotunda, near Vicenza.

♦ **1566** The Dutch revolt against the Spanish over the loss of political and religious freedoms:

Philip II of Spain sends 10,000 troops under the duke of Alba to suppress the revolt.

♦ **1569** Flemish cartographer Mercator produces a world map using a new projection.

♦ **1571** Philip II of Spain and an allied European force defeat the Ottomans at the battle of Lepanto.

♦ **1572** In Paris, France, a Catholic mob murders thousands of Huguenots in the Saint Bartholomew's Day Massacre.

♦ **1572** Danish astronomer Tycho Brahe sees a new star.

♦ **1573** Venetian artist Veronese paints the *Feast of the House of Levi*.

♦ **1579** The seven northern provinces of the Netherlands form the Union of Utrecht.

♦ **1580** Giambologna creates his mannerist masterpiece *Flying Mercury*.

♦ **1585** Henry III of France bans Protestantism in France; civil war breaks out again in the War of the Three Henrys.

♦ **1586** El Greco, a Greek artist active in Spain, paints the *Burial of Count Orgaz*.

♦ **1587** Mary, Queen of Scots, is executed by Elizabeth I of England.

♦ **c.1587** Nicholas Hilliard paints the miniature *Young Man among Roses*.

♦ **1588** Philip II of Spain launches his great Armada against England —but the fleet is destroyed.

♦ **1589** Henry of Navarre becomes king of France as Henry IV.

♦ **1592–1594** Tintoretto paints *The Last Supper*.

♦ **1596** Edmund Spencer publishes the *Faerie Queene*, glorifying Elizabeth I as "Gloriana."

♦ **1598** Henry IV of France grants Huguenots and Catholics equal political rights.

♦ **1598** In England the Globe Theater is built on London's south bank; it stages many of Shakespeare's plays.

♦ **1600–1601** Caravaggio paints *The Crucifixion of Saint Peter*, an early masterpiece of baroque art.

♦ **1603** Elizabeth I of England dies and is succeeded by James I, son of Mary, Queen of Scots.

♦ **1610** Galileo's *The Starry Messenger* supports the sun-centered model of the universe.

♦ **1620** The Italian painter Artemisia Gentileschi paints *Judith and Holofernes*.

Glossary

A.D. The letters A.D. stand for the Latin Anno Domini which means "in the year of our Lord." Dates with these letters written after them are measured forward from the year Christ was born.

Altarpiece A painting or sculpture placed behind an altar in a church.

Apprentice Someone (usually a young person) legally bound to a craftsman for a number of years in order to learn a craft.

B.C. Short for "Before Christ." Dates with these letters after them are measured backward from the year of Christ's birth.

Bureaucracy A system of government that relies on a body of officials and usually involves much paperwork and many regulations.

Cardinal An official of the Catholic church, highest in rank below the pope. The cardinals elect the pope.

Classical A term used to describe the civilizations of ancient Greece and Rome, and any later art and architecture based on ancient Greek and Roman examples.

Commission To order a specially made object, like a painting or tapestry.

Condottiere A mercenary soldier, that is, a soldier who will fight for anyone in return for money.

Contemporary Someone or something that lives or exists at the same period of time.

Curia The various offices in the Vatican that help the pope in his work as head of the Catholic church.

Diet A general assembly of representatives of the Holy Roman Empire who gathered together to make decisions and pass laws.

Draper A cloth merchant.

Edict A proclamation or order that has the force of law.

Entrepreneur A business person who is willing to take risks and try something new in order to make money.

Envoy Someone sent abroad to represent the government.

Equestrian A term used to describe something relating to a person on horseback. For example, an equestrian sculpture is a sculpture portraying a soldier or leader on horseback.

Excommunicate To ban someone from taking part in the rites of the church.

Foreshortening A technique used by artists to recreate the appearance of objects when seen from a particular angle. It involves shortening some measurements, according to the laws of perspective (see below), to make it look as if objects are projecting toward or receding away from the surface of the picture.

Fresco A type of painting that is usually used for decorating walls and ceilings in which colors are painted into wet plaster.

Guild An association of merchants or craftsmen organized to protect the interests of its members and to regulate the quality of their goods and services.

Heresy A belief that is contrary to the accepted teachings of the church.

Heretic Someone whose beliefs contradict the teachings of the church.

Humanism A new way of thinking about human life that characterized the Renaissance. It was based on the study of "humanities"— that is, ancient Greek and Roman texts, history, and philosophy—and stressed the importance of developing rounded, cultured people.

Hundred Years' War A long-drawn-out war between France and England, lasting from 1337 to 1453. It consisted of a series of campaigns with periods of tense peace in between.

Indulgences Cancelations of punishments for sins. Indulgences were often granted by the church in return for money.

Laity or lay people Anyone who is not a member of the clergy.

Mercenary A soldier who will fight for anyone in return for money.

Patron Someone who orders and pays for a work of art.

Patronage The act of ordering and paying for a work of art.

Perspective A technique that allows artists to create the impression of three-dimensional space in their pictures. Near objects are made to appear larger, and distant objects are shown as smaller.

Portico A term used in classical architecture to describe a roofed structure with columns and a triangular top on the front of a building; also known as a temple front.

Propaganda The spreading of ideas or information, true or false, in order to help a particular cause or person.

Seige A military blockade of a castle or a town to force it to surrender, often by cutting off its supplies of food and water.

Tempera A type of paint made by mixing powdered pigments (colors) with egg. Tempera was widely used by painters in medieval times and the Renaissance.

Treason The name given to a subject's act of betrayal of their king or queen.

Treatise A book or long essay about the principles, or rules, of a particular subject.

Triptych A picture or carving consisting of three panels side by side. It was often used as an altarpiece in churches and cathedrals.

Vassal A person who is bound to a local lord to whom they owe their loyalty and services.

Vatican The headquarters of the pope and papal government in Rome.

Vernacular The language of the ordinary people of a country, rather than a literary or formal language such as Latin.

Further Reading

Anderson, James Maxwell. *The History of Portugal*. Westport, CT: Greenwood Press, 2000.

Bainton, Roland Herbert. *Here I Stand: A Life of Martin Luther*. New York: Penguin USA, 1995.

Bainton, Roland Herbert. *The Reformation of the Sixteenth Century*. Boston, MA: Beacon Press, 1985.

Beck, James H. *Raphael*. New York: Harry N. Abrams, 1994.

Bedaux, Jan Baptist. *Rubens to Rembrandt: Children's Portraits in the Golden Age*. New York: Harry N. Abrams, 2001.

Bertelli, Carlo. *Piero della Francesca*. New Haven, CT: Yale University Press, 1992.

Boucher, Bruce. *Andrea Palladio: The Architect in His Time*. New York: Abbeville Press, 1998.

Brown, David Alan. *Virtue and Beauty: Leonardo's Ginevra de' Benci and Renaissance Portraits of Women*. Washington, DC: National Gallery of Art, 2001.

Brown, Howard Mayer, and Louise K. Stein. *Music in the Renaissance*. Upper Saddle River, NJ: Prentice Hall, 1999.

Burch, Joan Johansen. *Fine Print: A Story about Johann Gutenberg*. Minneapolis, MN: Carolrhoda Books, 1991.

Campbell, Lorne. *Renaissance Portraits: European Portrait Painting in the 14th, 15th, and 16th Centuries*. New Haven, CT: Yale University Press, 1990.

Cole, Alison. *Eyewitness Art: Perspective*. New York: DK Publishing, 1993.

De Hahn, Tracee. *The Black Death*. Broomall, PA: Chelsea House Publishing, 2001.

DK Art Books. *Piero della Francesca*. New York: DK Publishing, 1999.

Duffy, Eamon. *Saints and Sinners: A History of the Popes*. New Haven, CT: Yale University Press, 1999.

Dunn, Richard S. *The Age of Religious Wars, 1559–1715*. New York: W.W. Norton, 1980.

Elliott, John H. *Imperial Spain 1469–1716*. New York: Penguin USA, 1990.

Grierson, Edward. *King of Two Worlds: Philip II of Spain*. New York: Putnam, 1974.

Hoban, Sarah. *Daily Life in Ancient and Modern Paris*. Minneapolis, MN: Runestone Press, 2001.

Hollander, Robert. *Dante: A Life in Works*. New Haven, CT: Yale University Press, 2001.

Kamen, Henry Arthur Francis. *Philip of Spain*. New Haven, CT: Yale University Press, 1997.

Landau, David, and Peter Parshall. *The Renaissance Print: 1470–1550*. New Haven, CT: Yale University Press, 1994.

Lo Bello, Nino. *The Incredible Book of Vatican Facts and Papal Curiosities*. New York: Gramercy Books, 2002.

Mann, Nicholas, and Luke Syson. *The Image of the Individual: Portraits in the Renaissance*. London: British Museum Press, 1998.

Mattern, Joanne. *The Travels of Vasco da Gama*. Austin, TX: Raintree Steck-Vaughn, 2000.

McGowen, Tom. *The Black Death*. New York: Franklin Watts, 1995.

Merlo, Claudio. *Three Masters of the Renaissance: Leonardo, Michelangelo, Raphael*. Hauppauge, NY: Barron's Juveniles, 1999.

Morley, Jacqueline. *A Renaissance Town*. New York: Peter Bedrick Books, 1996.

Nardo, Don. *The Black Death*. San Diego, CA: Greenhaven Press, 1999.

Noll, Mark A. *Protestants in America*. Oxford: Oxford University Press Children's Books, 2000.

Oberhuber, Konrad. *Raphael: The Paintings*. New York: Prestel USA, 1999.

Perkins, Leeman L. *Music in the Age of the Renaissance*. New York: W.W. Norton, 1999.

Pettegree, Andrew. *The Reformation World*. London: Routledge, 2001.

Pollard, Michael, and Anna Sproule. *Johann Gutenberg: Master of Modern Printing*. Woodbridge, CT: Blackbirch Marketing, 2001.

Rice, Eugene F., Jr., and Anthony Santi, Bruno. *Raphael*. New York: Riverside Book Company, 1994.

Schneider, Norbert. *The Art of the Portrait*. New York: Taschen America, 1999.

Serafini-Sauli, Judith. *Giovanni Boccaccio*. Boston, MA: Twayne Publishers, 1982.

Smith, Ray. *DK Art School: An Introduction to Perspective*. New York: DK Publishing, 1995.

Stein, R. Conrad. *Paris*. New York: Children's Press, 1997.

Stepanek, Sally. *Calvin*. Broomall, PA: Chelsea House Publishing, 1987.

Stepanek, Sally. *Martin Luther*. Broomall, PA: Chelsea House Publishing, 1986.

Tavenor, Robert. *Palladio and Palladianism*. London: Thames & Hudson, 1991.

Venezia, Mike. *Raphael*. New York: Children's Press, 2001.

Wackernagel, Martin. *The World of the Florentine Renaissance Artist: Projects and Patrons, Workshop and Art Market*. Princeton, NJ: Princeton University Press, 1982.

Williams, Patrick. *Philip II*. New York: St. Martin's Press, 2001.

Wundram, Manfred, and Thomas Pape. *Andrea Palladio 1508–1580: Architect between the Renaissance and Baroque*. New York: Taschen America, 1996.

Zuffi, Stefano. *Dürer: Master Draftsman of the Renaissance—His Life in Paintings*. New York: DK Publishing, 1999.

WEBSITES

World history site
www.historyworld.net

BBC Online: History
www.bbc.co.uk/history

The Webmuseum's tour of the Renaissance
www.oir.ucf.edu/wm/paint/glo/renaissance/

Virtual time travel tour of the Renaissance
library.thinkquest.org/3588/Renaissance/

The Renaissance
www.learner.org/exhibits/renaissance

National Gallery of Art—tour of 16th-century Italian paintings
www.nga.gov/collection/gallery/ita16.htm

Uffizi Art Gallery, Florence
musa.uffizi.firenze.it/welcomeE.html

Database of Renaissance artists
www.artcyclopedia.com/index.html

Set Index

Picture Credits

MAPS
The maps in this book show the locations of cities, states, and empires of the
Renaissance period. However, for the sake of clarity, present-day place names are
often used.